New Perspectives on

Microsoft®
Word 97

BRIEF

Beverly B. Zimmerman

Brigham Young University

S. Scott Zimmerman

Brigham Young University

Ann Shaffer

A Susan Solomon Book

COURSE
TECHNOLOGY

ONE MAIN STREET, CAMBRIDGE, MA 02142

an International Thomson Publishing company I(T)P®

Cambridge • Albany • Bonn • Boston • Cincinnati • London • Madrid • Melbourne • Mexico City
New York • Paris • San Francisco • Singapore • Tokyo • Toronto • Washington

New Perspectives on Microsoft Word 97—Brief is published by Course Technology.

Associate Publisher	Mac Mendelsohn
Series Consulting Editor	Susan Solomon
Product Manager	Mark Reimold
Developmental Editor	Barbara Clemens
Technical Editor	Sasha Vodnik
Production Editor	Roxanne Alexander
Text and Cover Designer	Ella Hanna
Cover Illustrator	Douglas Goodman

© 1997 by Course Technology
A Division of International Thomson Publishing—I(T)P®

For more information contact:

Course Technology
One Main Street
Cambridge, MA 02142

International Thomson Editores
Campos Eliseos 385, Piso 7
Col. Polanco
11560 Mexico D.F. Mexico

International Thomson Publishing Europe
Berkshire House 168-173
High Holborn
London WCIV 7AA
England

International Thomson Publishing GmbH
Königswinterer Strasse 418
53227 Bonn
Germany

Thomas Nelson Australia
102 Dodds Street
South Melbourne, 3205
Victoria, Australia

International Thomson Publishing Asia
211 Henderson Road
#05-10 Henderson Building
Singapore 0315

Nelson Canada
1120 Birchmount Road
Scarborough, Ontario
Canada M1K 5G4

International Thomson Publishing Japan
Hirakawacho Kyowa Building, 3F
2-2-1 Hirakawacho
Chiyoda-ku, Tokyo 102
Japan

Trademarks
Course Technology and the Open Book logo are registered trademarks and CourseKits is a trademark of Course Technology. Custom Editions and the ITP logo are registered trademarks of International Thomson Publishing.

Some of the product names and company names used in this book have been used for identification purposes only and may be trademarks or registered trademarks of their respective manufacturers and sellers.

Disclaimer
Course Technology reserves the right to revise this publication and make changes from time to time in its content without notice.

ISBN 0-7600-4551-8

Printed in the United States of America

10 9 8 7 6 5 4 3

Preface The New Perspectives Series

What is the New Perspectives Series?

Course Technology's **New Perspectives Series** is an integrated system of instruction that combines text and technology products to teach computer concepts and micro-computer applications. Users consistently praise this series for innovative pedagogy, creativity, supportive and engaging style, accuracy, and use of interactive technology. The first New Perspectives text was published in January of 1993. Since then, the series has grown to more than 100 titles and has become the best-selling series on computer concepts and microcomputer applications. Others have imitated the New Perspectives features, design, and technologies, but none have replicated its quality and its ability to consistently anticipate and meet the needs of instructors and students.

How does this book I'm holding fit into the New Perspectives Series?

New Perspectives applications books are available in the following categories:

Brief books are typically about 160 pages long, contain two to four tutorials, and are intended to teach the basics of an application. The book you are holding is a Brief book.

Introductory books are typically about 300 pages long and consist of four to seven tutorials that go beyond the basics. These books often build out of the Brief editions by providing two or three additional tutorials.

Comprehensive books are typically about 600 pages long and consist of all of the tutorials in the Introductory books, plus four or five more tutorials covering higher-level topics. Comprehensive books also include two Windows tutorials, three or four Additional Cases, and a Reference Section.

Advanced books cover topics similar to those in the Comprehensive books, but go into more depth. Advanced books present the most high-level coverage in the series.

Custom Books The New Perspectives Series offers you two ways to customize a New Perspectives text to fit your course exactly: *CourseKits*™, two or more texts packaged together in a box, and *Custom Editions*®, your choice of books bound together. Custom Editions offer you unparalleled flexibility in designing your concepts and applications courses. You can build your own book by ordering a combination of titles bound together to cover only the topics you want. Your students save because they buy only the materials they need. There is no minimum order, and books are spiral bound. Both CourseKits and Custom Editions offer significant price discounts. Contact your Course Technology sales representative for more information.

New Perspectives Series Microcomputer Applications

- Brief Titles or Modules
- Introductory Titles or Modules
- Intermediate Tutorials
- Advanced Titles or Modules
- Other Modules

Brief	Introductory	Comprehensive	Advanced	Custom Editions
2 to 4 tutorials	6 or 7 tutorials, or Brief + 2 or 3 more tutorials	Introductory + 4 or 5 more tutorials. Includes Brief Windows tutorials, Additional Cases, and References section	Quick Review of basics + in-depth, high-level coverage	Choose from any of the above to build your own Custom Editions® or CourseKits™

How do the Windows 95 editions differ from the Windows 3.1 editions?

SESSION 1.1

Sessions We've divided the tutorials into sessions. Each session is designed to be completed in about 45 minutes to an hour (depending, of course, upon student needs and the speed of your lab equipment). With sessions, learning is broken up into more easily-assimilated portions. You can more accurately allocate time in your syllabus, and students can better manage the available lab time. Each session begins with a "session box," which quickly describes the skills students will learn in the session. Furthermore, each session is numbered, which makes it easier for you and your students to navigate and communicate about the tutorial. Look on page W 1.5 for the session box that opens Session 1.1.

Quick Check

Quick Checks Each session concludes with meaningful, conceptual Quick Check questions that test students' understanding of what they learned in the session. Answers to all of the Quick Check questions in this book are provided on pages W 4.31 through W 4.35.

New Design We have retained the best of the old design to help students differentiate between what they are to *do* and what they are to *read*. The steps are clearly identified by their shaded background and numbered steps. Furthermore, this new design presents steps and screen shots in a larger, easier to read format. Some good examples of our new design are pages W 2.4 and W 2.5.

What features are retained in the Windows 95 editions of the New Perspectives Series?

"Read This Before You Begin" Page This page is consistent with Course Technology's unequaled commitment to helping instructors introduce technology into the classroom. Technical considerations and assumptions about software are listed to help instructors save time and eliminate unnecessary aggravation. The page also provides important information about Student Disks. See page W 1.2 for the "Read This Before You Begin" page in this book.

CASE

Tutorial Case Each tutorial begins with a problem presented in a case that is meaningful to students. The problem turns the task of learning how to use an application into a problem-solving process. The problems increase in complexity with each tutorial. These cases touch on multicultural, international, and ethical issues—so important to today's business curriculum. See page W 1.3 for the case that begins Tutorial 1.

1. 2. 3.

Step-by-Step Methodology This unique Course Technology methodology keeps students on track. They enter data, click buttons, or press keys always within the context of solving the problem posed in the tutorial case. The text constantly guides students, letting them know where they are in the course of solving the problem. In addition, the numerous screen shots include labels that direct students' attention to what they should look at on the screen. On almost every page in this book, you can find an example of how steps, screen shots, and labels work together.

TROUBLE?

TROUBLE? Paragraphs These paragraphs anticipate the mistakes or problems that students are likely to have and help them recover and continue with the tutorial. By putting these paragraphs in the book, rather than in the Instructor's Manual, we facilitate independent learning and free the instructor to focus on substantive conceptual issues rather than on common procedural errors. Two representative examples of TROUBLE? paragraphs are on pages W 2.10 and W 2.22.

Reference Windows Reference Windows appear throughout the text. They are succinct summaries of the most important tasks covered in the tutorials. Reference Windows are specially designed and written so students can refer to them when doing the Tutorial Assignments and Case Problems, and after completing the course. Page W 2.9 contains the Reference Window for Dragging and Dropping Text.

Task Reference The Task Reference contains a summary of how to perform common tasks using the most efficient method, as well as references to pages where the task is discussed in more detail. It appears as a table at the end of the book.

Tutorial Assignments, Case Problems, and Lab Assignments Each tutorial concludes with Tutorial Assignments, which provide students with additional hands-on practice of the skills they learned in the tutorial. See page W 4.25 for examples of Tutorial Assignments. The Tutorial Assignments are followed by four Case Problems that have approximately the same scope as the tutorial case. In the Windows 95 applications texts, the last Case Problem of each tutorial typically requires students to solve the problem independently, either "from scratch" or with minimum guidance. See page W 3.32 for examples of Case Problems. Finally, if a Course Lab accompanies a tutorial, Lab Assignments are included after the Case Problems. See page W 1.31 for the Word Processing Lab Assignments.

Exploration Exercises The Windows environment allows students to learn by exploring and discovering what they can do. Exploration Exercises can be Tutorial Assignments or Case Problems that challenge students, encourage them to explore the capabilities of the program they are using, and extend their knowledge using the Help facility and other reference materials. Page W 3.30 contains Exploration Exercises for Tutorial 3.

What supplements are available with this textbook?

Course Labs: Now, Concepts Come to Life Computer skills and concepts come to life with the New Perspectives Course Labs—highly-interactive tutorials that combine illustrations, animations, digital images, and simulations. The Labs guide students step-by-step, present them with Quick Check questions, let them explore on their own, test their comprehension, and provide printed feedback. Lab icons at the beginning of the tutorial and in the tutorial margins indicate when a topic has a corresponding Lab. Lab Assignments are included at the end of each relevant tutorial. The Lab available with this book and the tutorial in which it appears is:

TUTORIAL 1

Course Test Manager: Testing and Practice at the Computer or on Paper Course Test Manager is cutting-edge Windows-based testing software that helps instructors design and administer practice tests and actual examinations. This full-featured program allows students to randomly generate practice tests that provide immediate on-screen feedback and detailed study guides. Instructors can also use Course Test Manager to produce printed tests. Course Test Manager can automatically grade the tests students take at the computer and can generate statistical information on individual as well as group performance.

Online Companions: Dedicated to Keeping You and Your Students Up-To-Date When you use a New Perspectives product, you can access Course Technology's faculty sites and student sites on the World Wide Web. You can browse the password-protected Faculty Online Companions to obtain online Instructor's Manuals, Solution Files, Student Files, and more. Please see your Instructor's Manual or call your Course Technology customer service representative for more information. Student and Faculty Online Companions are accessible by clicking the appropriate links on Course Technology's home page at **http://www.course.com**.

Instructor's Manual New Perspectives Series Instructor's Manuals contain instructor's notes and printed solutions for each tutorial. Instructor's notes provide tutorial overviews and outlines, technical notes, lecture notes, and extra Case Problems. Printed solutions include solutions to Tutorial Assignments, Case Problems, and Lab Assignments.

Internet Assignments The Instructor's Manual that accompanies this book includes additional assignments that integrate the World Wide Web with the word processing skills students learn in the tutorials. To complete these assignments, students will need to search the Web and follow the links from the New Perspectives on Microsoft Office 97 home page. The Office 97 home page is accessible through the Student Online Companions link found on the Course Technology home page at **http://www.course.com**. Please refer to the Instructor's Manual for more information.

Student Files Student Files contain all of the data that students will use to complete the tutorials, Tutorial Assignments, and Case Problems. A Readme file includes technical tips for lab management. See the inside covers of this book and the "Read This Before You Begin" page before Tutorial 1 for more information on Student Files.

Solution Files Solution Files contain every file students are asked to create or modify in the tutorials, Tutorial Assignments, and Case Problems.

The following supplements are included in the Instructor's Resource Kit that accompanies this textbook:

- Instructor's Manual
- Solution Files
- Student Files
- Word Processing Course Lab
- Course Test Manager Release 1.1 Test Bank
- Course Test Manager Release 1.1 Engine

Some of the supplements listed above are also available over the World Wide Web through Course Technology's password-protected Faculty Online Companions. Please see your Instructor's Manual or call your Course Technology customer service representative for more information.

Acknowledgments

We would like to acknowledge the invaluable contributions of our reviewers: Nancy Alderdice, Murray State University; Maureen Duncan, Vista College, and Grant Getz, Arizona State University. We sincerely thank Developmental Editor Barbara Clemens for her thorough editing, clear writing, and thoughtful suggestions; Technical Editor Sasha Vodnik for his software know-how, careful work, and many fine ideas, Quality Assurance Project Leader Greg Bigelow for coordinating the testing process, and John McCarthy for his conscientious quality assurance testing. Also our thanks to Mark Reimold for helping us maintain series consistency and answering all of our questions; to Roxanne Alexander for her excellent production work; to Jane Pedicini for her fine copy editing; to Lisa Rappa for her thorough proofreading and Editorial Assistant Rachel Crapser for her help during every phase of this book's development.

Beverly B. Zimmerman
S. Scott Zimmerman
Ann Shaffer

Microsoft® Word 97

LEVEL I

TUTORIALS

Read This **Before You Begin**

STUDENT DISK

To complete Word 97 Tutorials 1-4, you need a Student Disk. Your instructor will either provide you with a Student Disk or ask you to make your own.

If you are supposed to make your own Student Disk, you will need one blank, formatted, high-density disk. You will need to copy a set of folders from a file server or standalone computer onto your disk. Your instructor will tell you which computer, drive letter, and folders contain the files you need. The following table shows you which folders go on your disk:

Student Disk	Write this on the disk label	Put these folders on the disk
1	Student Disk 1: Word 97 Tutorials 1-4	Tutorial.01, Tutorial.02, Tutorial.03, Tutorial.04

See the inside front or inside back cover of this book for more information on Student Disk files, or ask your instructor or technical support person for assistance.

COURSE LAB

Tutorial 1 features an interactive Course Lab to help you understand word processing concepts. There are Lab Assignments at the end of the tutorial that relate to this Lab. To start the Lab, click the Start button on the Windows 95 Taskbar, point to Programs, point to Course Labs, point to New Perspectives Applications, and click Word Processing.

USING YOUR OWN COMPUTER

If you are going to work through this book using your own computer, you need:
- **Computer System** Microsoft Windows 95 or Microsoft Windows NT Workstation 4.0 (or a later version) and Microsoft Word 97 must be installed on your computer. This book assumes a typical installation of Microsoft Word 97.
- **Student Disk** Ask your instructor or lab manager for details on how to get the Student Disk. You will not be able to complete the tutorials or end-of-tutorial assignments in this book using your own computer until you have a Student Disk. The Student Files may also be obtained electronically over the Internet. See the inside front or inside back cover of this book for more details.
- **Course Lab** See your instructor or technical support person to obtain the Course Lab software for use on your own computer.

To complete Word 97 Tutorials 1-4, your students must use a set of files on a Student Disk. These files are included in the Instructor's Resource Kit, and they may also be obtained electronically over the Internet. See the inside front or inside back cover of this book for more details. Follow the instructions in the Readme file to copy the files to your server or standalone computer. You can view the Readme file using WordPad. Once the files are copied, you can make Student Disks for the students yourself, or you can tell students where to find the files so they can make their own Student Disks.

COURSE LAB SOFTWARE

The Course Lab software is distributed on a CD-ROM included in the Instructor's Resource Kit. To install the Course Lab software, follow the setup instructions in the Readme file on the CD-ROM. Refer also to the Readme file for essential technical notes related to running the Lab in a multi-user environment. Once you have installed the Course Lab software, your students can start the Lab from the Windows 95 desktop by following the instructions in the Course Labs section above.

COURSE TECHNOLOGY STUDENT FILES AND LAB SOFTWARE

You are granted a license to copy the Student Files and Lab software to any computer or computer network used by students who have purchased this book.

Creating a Document

Writing a Business Letter for Crossroads

OBJECTIVES

In this tutorial you will:

- Start and exit Word

- Identify the components of the Word window

- Choose commands using the toolbars and menus

- Correct spelling errors with AutoCorrect

- Scroll through a document

- Create, save, and print a document

- Use the Word Help system to get Help

LABS

Word
Processing

CASE

Crossroads

Karen Liu is executive director of Crossroads, a small, non-profit organization in Tacoma, Washington. Crossroads distributes business clothing to low-income clients who are returning to the job market or starting new careers. To make potential clients in the community more aware of their services, Crossroads reserves an exhibit booth each year at a local job fair sponsored by the Tacoma Chamber of Commerce. Crossroads needs to find out the date and location of this year's fair, as well as some other logistical information, before they can reserve a booth. Karen asks you to write a letter requesting this information from the Tacoma Chamber of Commerce.

In this tutorial you will create Karen's letter using Microsoft Word 97, a popular word-processing program. Before you begin typing the letter, you will learn to start the Word program, identify and use the elements of the Word screen, and adjust some Word settings. You will then go on to create a new Word document, type in the text of the Crossroads letter, save the letter, and then print the letter for Karen. In the process of entering the text, you'll learn several ways of correcting typing errors. You'll also learn how to use the Word Help system, which allows you to quickly find answers to your questions about the program.

Using the Tutorials Effectively

These tutorials are designed to be used at a computer. Each tutorial is divided into sessions. Watch for the session headings, such as "Session 1.1" and "Session 1.2." Each session is designed to be completed in about 45 minutes, but take as much time as you need. When you've completed a session, it's a good idea to exit the program and take a break. You can exit Microsoft Word by clicking the Close button in the top-right corner of the program window.

Before you begin, read the following questions and answers. They are designed to help you use the tutorials effectively.

Where do I start?

Each tutorial begins with a case, which sets the scene for the tutorial and gives you background information to help you understand what you will be doing in the tutorial. Read the case before you go to the lab. In the lab, begin with the first session of the tutorial.

How do I know what to do on the computer?

Each session contains steps that you will perform on the computer to learn how to use Microsoft Word. The steps are numbered and are set against a colored background. Read the text that introduces each series of steps, and read each step carefully and completely before you try it.

How do I know if I did the step correctly?

As you work, compare your computer screen with the corresponding figure in the tutorial. Don't worry if your screen display is somewhat different from the figure. The important parts of the screen display are labeled in each figure. Check to make sure these parts are on your screen.

What if I make a mistake?

Don't worry about making mistakes—they are part of the learning process. Paragraphs labeled "TROUBLE?" identify common problems and explain how to get back on track. Follow the steps in a TROUBLE? paragraph *only* if you are having the problem described. If you run into other problems, carefully consider the current state of your system, the position of the pointer, and any messages on the screen.

How do I use the Reference Windows?

Reference Windows summarize the procedures you learn in the tutorial steps. Do not complete the actions in the Reference Windows when you are working through the tutorial. Instead, refer to the Reference Windows while you are working on the assignments at the end of the tutorial.

How can I test my understanding of the material I learned in the tutorial?

At the end of each session, you can answer the Quick Check questions. If necessary, refer to the Answers to Quick Check Questions to check your work.

After you have completed the entire tutorial, you should complete the Tutorial Assignments and Case Problems. These exercises are carefully structured so you will review what you have learned and then apply your knowledge to new situations.

What if I can't remember how to do something?

You should refer to the Task Reference at the end of the book; it summarizes how to accomplish commonly performed tasks.

What is the Word Processing Course Lab, and how should I use it?

This interactive Lab helps you review word processing concepts and practice skills that you learn in Tutorial 1. The Lab Assignments section at the end of Tutorial 1 includes instructions for using the Lab.

Now that you've seen how to use the tutorials effectively, you are ready to begin.

In this session you will learn how to start Word, how to identify and use the parts of the Word screen, and how to adjust some Word settings. With the skills you learn in this session, you'll be prepared to use Word to create a variety of documents, such as letters, reports, and memos.

Four Steps to a Professional Document

Word helps you produce quality work in minimal time. Not only can you type a document, you can quickly make editing changes and corrections, adjust margins and spacing, create columns and tables, and add graphics to your documents. The most efficient way to produce a document is to follow these four steps: 1) planning and creating, 2) editing, 3) formatting, and 4) printing.

In the long run, *planning* saves you time and effort. First, you should determine what you want to say. State your purpose clearly and include enough information to achieve that purpose without overwhelming or boring your reader. Be sure to *organize* your ideas logically. Also, decide how you want your document to look—its *presentation*. In this case, your letter to the Tacoma Chamber of Commerce will take the form of a standard business letter. Karen has given you a handwritten note with all her questions for the Tacoma Chamber of Commerce, as shown in Figure 1-1.

Figure 1-1 ◀
Karen's
questions about
the job fair

> Please write the Tacoma Chamber of Commerce and find out the following:
>
> What are the location and dates for this year's job fair?
>
> Is a map of the exhibit area available? What size booths are available and how can we reserve a booth?
>
> Who do we contact about what physical facilities are available at each booth?
>
> Send the letter to the Chamber's president. The address is 210 Shoreline Vista, Suite 1103, Tacoma WA 98402.

After you've planned your document, you can go ahead and *create* it using Word. The next step, *editing*, consists of reading through the document you've created, then correcting your errors, and finally adding or deleting text to make the document easy to read.

Once your document is error-free, you can *format* it to make it visually appealing. As you'll learn in Tutorial 2, formatting features, such as white space (blank areas of a page), line spacing, boldface, and italics can help make your document easier to read. *Printing* is the final phase in creating an effective document. In this tutorial, you will preview your document before you spend time and resources to print it.

Starting Word

Before you can apply these four steps to produce the letter using Word, you need to start Word and learn about the general organization of the Word screen. You'll do that now.

To start Microsoft Word:

1. Make sure Windows 95 is running on your computer and the Windows 95 desktop appears on your screen.

   TROUBLE? If you're running Windows NT Workstation 4.0 (or a later version) on your computer or network, don't worry. Although the figures in this book were created while running Windows 95, Windows NT 4.0 and Windows 95 share the same interface, and Word 97 runs equally well under either operating system.

2. Click the **Start** button on the taskbar to display the Start menu, and then point to **Programs** to display the Programs menu.

3. Point to **Microsoft Word** on the Programs menu. See Figure 1-2.

Figure 1-2 ◀
Starting
Microsoft Word

position mouse
pointer here to open
Programs menu

Start button

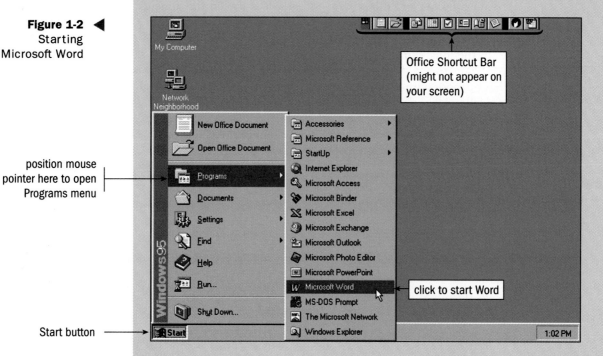

   TROUBLE? If you don't see the Microsoft Word option on the Programs menu, ask your instructor or technical support person for help.

   TROUBLE? The Office Shortcut Bar, which appears along the top border of the desktop in Figure 1-2, might look different on your screen, or it might not appear at all, depending on how your system is set up. Since the Office Shortcut Bar is not required to complete these tutorials, it has been omitted from the remaining figures in this text.

4. Click **Microsoft Word**. After a short pause, the Microsoft Word copyright information appears in a message box and remains on the screen until the Word program window, containing a blank Word document, is displayed. See Figure 1-3.

Word

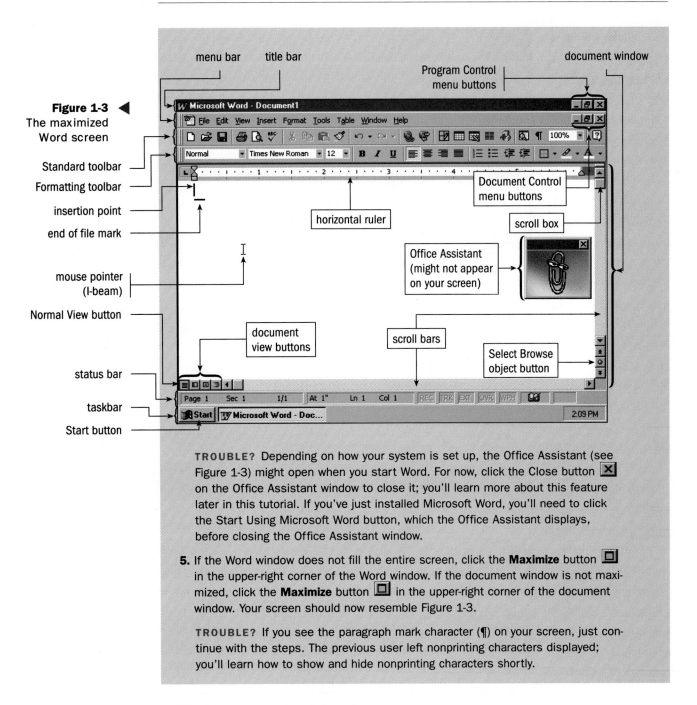

Figure 1-3 ◄
The maximized
Word screen

Standard toolbar
Formatting toolbar
insertion point
end of file mark

mouse pointer
(I-beam)

Normal View button

status bar

taskbar

Start button

menu bar   title bar   document window

Program Control
menu buttons

Document Control
menu buttons

horizontal ruler

scroll box

Office Assistant
(might not appear
on your screen)

document
view buttons

scroll bars

Select Browse
object button

TROUBLE? Depending on how your system is set up, the Office Assistant (see Figure 1-3) might open when you start Word. For now, click the Close button ⊠ on the Office Assistant window to close it; you'll learn more about this feature later in this tutorial. If you've just installed Microsoft Word, you'll need to click the Start Using Microsoft Word button, which the Office Assistant displays, before closing the Office Assistant window.

5. If the Word window does not fill the entire screen, click the **Maximize** button ▢ in the upper-right corner of the Word window. If the document window is not maximized, click the **Maximize** button ▢ in the upper-right corner of the document window. Your screen should now resemble Figure 1-3.

TROUBLE? If you see the paragraph mark character (¶) on your screen, just continue with the steps. The previous user left nonprinting characters displayed; you'll learn how to show and hide nonprinting characters shortly.

Word is now running and ready to use.

The Word Screen

The Word screen is made up of both a program window and a document window. The **program window**, also called the Word window, opens automatically when you start Word and contains all the toolbars and menus. The **document window**, which opens within the Word window, is where you type and edit documents.

Figure 1-3 shows the Word screen with both windows maximized. If your screen doesn't look exactly like Figure 1-3, just continue for now. Figure 1-4 lists each element of the Word screen and summarizes its function. You are already familiar with some of these elements, such as the menu bar, title bar, and status bar, because they are common to all Windows screens.

Figure 1-4
Summary
of functions of
Word screen

Screen Element	Function
Title bar	Identifies the current application (i.e., Microsoft Word); shows the filename of the current document
Control menu buttons	Program Control menu buttons size and close the Word window; Document Control menu buttons size and close the current document window
Menu bar	Contains lists or menus of all the Word commands
Standard toolbar	Contains buttons to activate frequently used commands
Formatting toolbar	Contains buttons to activate common font and paragraph formatting commands
Select Browse object button	Displays buttons that allow you to move quickly through the document
Horizontal ruler	Adjusts margins, tabs, and column widths; vertical ruler appears in page layout view
Document window	Area where you enter text and graphics
Document view buttons	Show document in four different views: normal view, online layout view, page layout view, and outline view
Status bar	Provides information regarding the location of the insertion point
Taskbar	Shows programs that are running and allows you to switch quickly from one program to another
Mouse pointer	Changes shape depending on its location on the screen (i.e., I-beam pointer in text area; arrow in nontext areas)
Insertion point	Indicates location where characters will be inserted or deleted
Scroll bars	Shift text vertically and horizontally on the screen so you can see different parts of the document
Scroll box	Helps you move quickly to other pages of your document
Start button	Starts a program, opens a document, provides quick access to Windows 95 Help

If at any time you would like to check the name of a Word toolbar button, just position the mouse pointer over the button without clicking. A **ScreenTip**, a small yellow box with the name of the button, will appear.

Checking the Screen Before You Begin Each Tutorial

Word provides a set of standard settings, called **default settings**, that are appropriate for most documents. The setup of your Word document might have different default settings from those shown in the figures. This often happens when you share a computer and another user changes the appearance of the Word screen. The rest of this section explains what your screen should look like and how to make it match those in the tutorials.

Setting the Document View to Normal

You can view your document in one of four ways—normal, online layout, page layout, or outline. **Online layout** and **outline view** are designed for special situations that you don't need to worry about now. You will, however, learn more about **page layout view**—which allows you to see a page's design and format—in later tutorials. In most cases you'll want to use **normal view** when completing these tutorials. Depending on the document view selected by the last person who used Word, you might need to change the document back to normal view.

To make sure the document window is in normal view:

1. Click the **Normal View** button ▤ to the left of the horizontal scroll bar. See Figure 1-5. If your document window was not in normal view, it changes to normal view now.

Figure 1-5 ◄
Changing to
normal view

Normal View button ————

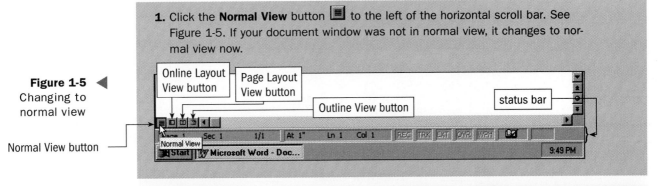

Displaying the Toolbars and Ruler

These tutorials frequently use the Standard toolbar and the Formatting toolbar to help you work more efficiently. Each time you start Word, check to make sure both toolbars appear on your screen. If either toolbar is missing, or if other toolbars are displayed, perform the steps below.

To display or hide a toolbar:

1. Position the pointer over any visible toolbar and click the right mouse button. A shortcut menu appears. The menu lists all available toolbars, and displays a check mark next to those currently displayed.

2. If the Standard or Formatting toolbar is not visible, click its name on the shortcut menu to place a check mark next to it. If any toolbars besides the Formatting and Standard toolbars have checkmarks, click each one to remove the check mark and hide the toolbar.

As you complete these tutorials, the ruler should also be visible to help you place items precisely. If your ruler is not visible, perform the next step.

To display the ruler:

1. Click **View** on the menu bar, and then click **Ruler** to place a check mark next to it.

Setting the Font and Font Size

A **font** is a set of characters that has a certain design, shape, and appearance. Each font has a name, such as Courier, Times New Roman, or Arial. The **font size** is the actual height of a character, measured in points, where one point equals $\frac{1}{72}$ of an inch in height. You'll learn more about fonts and font sizes in Tutorial 2, but for now simply keep in mind that most of the documents you'll create will use the Times New Roman font in a font size of 12 points. Word usually uses a default setting of 10-point font size in new documents. This font size, however, is not as easy to read as the larger 12-point font. If your font setting is not Times New Roman 12 point, you should change the default setting now. You'll use the menu bar to choose the desired commands.

To change the default font and font size:

1. Click **Format** on the menu bar, and then click **Font** to open the Font dialog box. If necessary, click the Font tab. See Figure 1-6.

Figure 1-6 ◀
Font dialog box

use this font ————▶

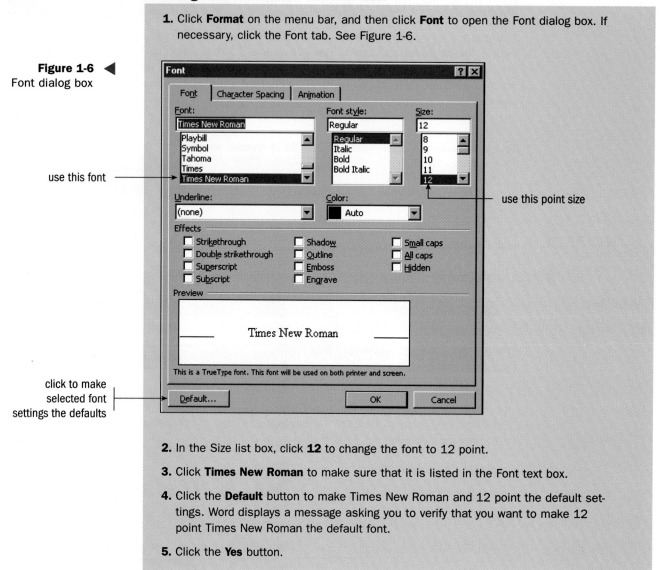

use this point size

click to make
selected font
settings the defaults

2. In the Size list box, click **12** to change the font to 12 point.

3. Click **Times New Roman** to make sure that it is listed in the Font text box.

4. Click the **Default** button to make Times New Roman and 12 point the default settings. Word displays a message asking you to verify that you want to make 12 point Times New Roman the default font.

5. Click the **Yes** button.

Displaying Nonprinting Characters

Nonprinting characters are symbols that can be displayed on the screen but that do not show up when you print your document. You can display them when you are working on the appearance, or **format**, of your document. For example, one nonprinting character marks the end of a paragraph (¶), while another marks the space between words (•). It's sometimes helpful to display nonprinting characters so you can actually see whether you've typed an extra space, ended a paragraph, typed spaces instead of tabs, and so on. In general, in these tutorials, you will display nonprinting characters only when you are formatting a document. You'll display them now, though, so you can use them as guides when typing your first letter.

To display nonprinting characters:

1. Click the **Show/Hide ¶** button ¶ on the Standard toolbar to display the nonprinting characters. A paragraph mark (¶) appears at the top of the document window. See Figure 1-7.

Figure 1-7 ◀
Nonprinting
characters
activated

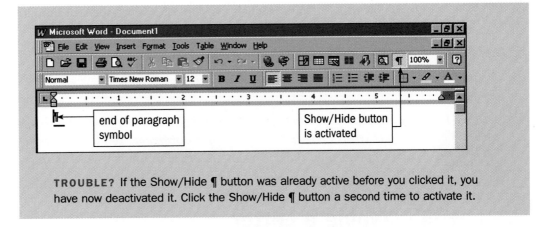

TROUBLE? If the Show/Hide ¶ button was already active before you clicked it, you have now deactivated it. Click the Show/Hide ¶ button a second time to activate it.

To make sure your screen always matches the figures in this book, remember to complete the checklist in Figure 1-8 each time you sit down at the computer.

Figure 1-8 ◀
Word screen
session
checklist

Screen Element	Setting	Check
Document view	Normal	
Program and document windows	Maximized	
Standard toolbar	Displayed	
Formatting toolbar	Displayed	
Other toolbars	Hidden	
Nonprinting characters	Hidden	
Font	Times New Roman	
Point size	12 point	
Ruler	Displayed	

Quick Check

1 In your own words, list and describe the steps in creating a document.

2 How do you start Word from the Windows 95 desktop?

3 Define each of the following in your own words:
   a. Standard toolbar
   b. ruler
   c. insertion point
   d. font
   e. default settings

4 How do you change the default font size?

5 How do you display or hide the Standard toolbar?

6 How do you display or hide nonprinting characters?

Now that you have planned a document, opened the Word program, identified screen elements, and adjusted settings, you are ready to create a new document. In the next session, you will create Karen's letter to the Tacoma Chamber of Commerce.

SESSION

1.2

In this session you will create a one-page document using Word. You'll learn how to correct errors and scroll through your document. You'll also learn how to name, save, preview, and print the document, and how to use the Word Help system.

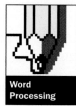

Word Processing

Typing a Letter

You're ready to type Karen's letter to the Tacoma Chamber of Commerce. Figure 1-9 shows the completed letter printed on the company letterhead. You'll begin by opening a new blank page (in case you accidentally typed something in the current page). Then you'll move the insertion point to about 2½ inches from the top margin of the paper to allow space for the Crossroads letterhead.

Figure 1-9 ◀
Job fair letter

crossroads

1414 East Bellingham S.W.
Suite 318
Tacoma, WA 98402

February 21, 1998

Deborah Brown, President
Tacoma Chamber of Commerce
210 Shoreline Vista, Suite 1103
Tacoma, WA 98402

Dear Deborah:

Recently, you contacted our staff about the Chamber's decision to sponsor a job fair again this year. We are interested in participating as we have done in the past.

Please send us information about the dates and location for this year's fair. If a map of the exhibit area is available, we would appreciate receiving a copy of it. Also, please send us the name and address of someone we can contact regarding the on-site physical facilities. Specifically, we need to know what size the exhibit booths are and how we can reserve one.

Thank you for your help in this matter. We look forward to participating in the job fair and hope to hear from you soon.

Sincerely yours,

Karen Liu
Executive Director

To open a new document:

1. If you took a break after the last session, make sure the Word program is running, that nonprinting characters are displayed, and that the font settings in the Formatting toolbar are set to 12 point Times New Roman.

2. Click the **New** button 🗋 on the Standard toolbar to open a new, blank document.

3. Press the **Enter** key eight times. Each time you press the Enter key, a nonprinting paragraph mark appears. In the status bar (at the bottom of the document window) you should see the setting "At 2.5"", indicating that the insertion point is 2½ inches from the top of the page. Another setting in the status bar should read "Ln 9", indicating the insertion point is in line 9 of the document. See Figure 1-10.

Figure 1-10 ◀
Document
window after
inserting
blank lines

insertion point
at 2.5 inches

line number

vertical location

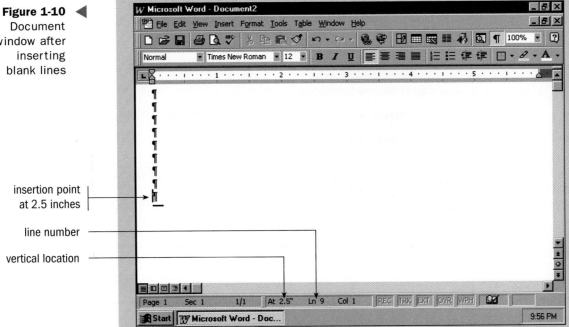

TROUBLE? If the paragraph mark doesn't appear each time you press the Enter key, the nonprinting characters might be hidden. To show the nonprinting characters, click the Show/Hide ¶ button ⊡.

TROUBLE? If you pressed the Enter key too many times, just press the Backspace key to delete each extra line and paragraph mark. If you're on line 9 but the At number is not 2.5", don't worry. Different fonts and monitors produce slightly different measurements when you press the Enter key.

Using AutoText Tips

Now you're ready to type the date. As you do it, you'll take advantage of Word's **AutoText** feature, which automatically types dates and other regularly used words and text for you.

To insert the date using an AutoText tip:

1. Type **Febr** (the first four letters of February). An AutoText tip appears above the line, as shown in Figure 1-11.

Figure 1-11 ◀
AutoText tip

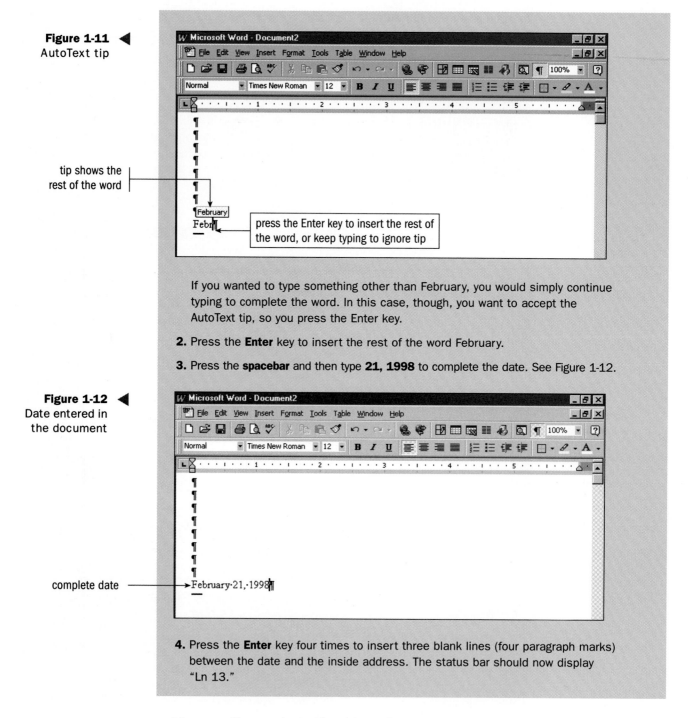

tip shows the
rest of the word

press the Enter key to insert the rest of
the word, or keep typing to ignore tip

If you wanted to type something other than February, you would simply continue
typing to complete the word. In this case, though, you want to accept the
AutoText tip, so you press the Enter key.

2. Press the **Enter** key to insert the rest of the word February.

3. Press the **spacebar** and then type **21, 1998** to complete the date. See Figure 1-12.

Figure 1-12 ◀
Date entered in
the document

complete date

February·21,·1998¶

4. Press the **Enter** key four times to insert three blank lines (four paragraph marks)
between the date and the inside address. The status bar should now display
"Ln 13."

Next, you'll enter the inside address shown on Karen's note.

Entering Text

You'll enter the inside address by typing it. If you type a wrong character, simply press the
Backspace key to delete the mistake and then retype it.

To type the inside address:

1. Type **Deborah Brown, President** and press the **Enter** key. As you type, the nonprinting character (•) appears between words to indicate a space.

Word

TROUBLE? If a wavy red or green line appears beneath a word, check to make sure you typed the text correctly. If you did not, use the Backspace key to remove the error, and then retype the text correctly.

2. Type the following text, pressing the **Enter** key after each line to enter the inside address.

   Tacoma Chamber of Commerce
   210 Shoreline Vista, Suite 1103
   Tacoma, WA 98402

3. Press the **Enter** key again to add a blank line between the inside address and the salutation. See Figure 1-13.

Figure 1-13 ◄
Document
window
showing inside
address

inside address ——

extra blank line ——

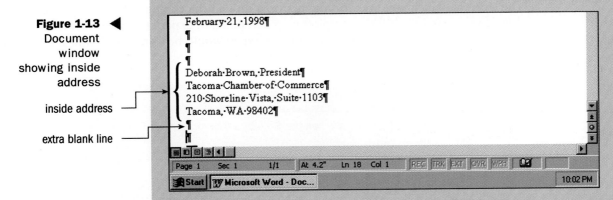

4. Type **Dear Deborah:** and press the **Enter** key twice to double space between the salutation and the body of the letter.

   When you press the Enter key the first time, the Office Assistant appears and asks if you would like help writing your letter. See Figure 1-14.

Figure 1-14 ◄
Office
Assistant

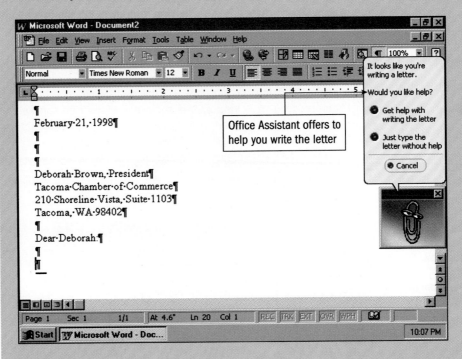

Office Assistant offers to help you write the letter

The Office Assistant is a special feature that sometimes appears to offer help on routine tasks. In this case, you could click the "Get help with writing the letter button" and have the Office Assistant lead you through a series of dialog boxes designed to set up the basic elements of your letter automatically. You'll learn more about the

Office Assistant later in this tutorial. Then, in the Tutorial Assignments, you'll have a chance to create a letter with the help of the Office Assistant. For now, though, you'll close the Office Assistant and continue writing your letter.

5. Click the **Just type the letter without help** button to close the Office Assistant.

You have completed the date, the inside address, and the salutation of Karen's letter, using a standard business letter format. You're ready to complete the letter. Before you do, however, you should save what you have typed so far.

Saving a Document

The letter on which you are working is stored only in the computer's memory, not on a disk. If you were to exit Word, turn off your computer, or experience an accidental power failure, the part of Karen's letter that you just typed would be lost. You should get in the habit of frequently saving your document to a disk.

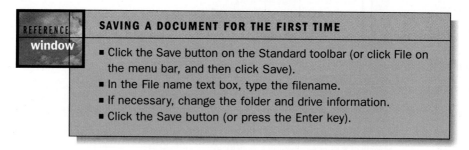

REFERENCE window	**SAVING A DOCUMENT FOR THE FIRST TIME**
	■ Click the Save button on the Standard toolbar (or click File on the menu bar, and then click Save).
	■ In the File name text box, type the filename.
	■ If necessary, change the folder and drive information.
	■ Click the Save button (or press the Enter key).

After you name your document, Word automatically appends the .doc filename extension to identify the file as a Microsoft Word document. However, depending on how Windows 95 is set up (or configured) on your computer, you might not actually see .doc extension. These tutorials assume that filename extensions are hidden.

To save the document:

1. Place your Student Disk in the appropriate disk drive.

TROUBLE? If you don't have a Student Disk, you need to get one before you can proceed. Your instructor or technical support person will either give you one or ask you to make your own by following the instructions on the "Read This Before You Begin" page at the beginning of this tutorial. See your instructor or technical support person for more information.

2. Click the **Save** button 🖫 on the Standard toolbar. The Save As dialog box opens. See Figure 1-15.

Figure 1-15 ◀
Save As
dialog box

change folder to
Tutorial.01

type filename here

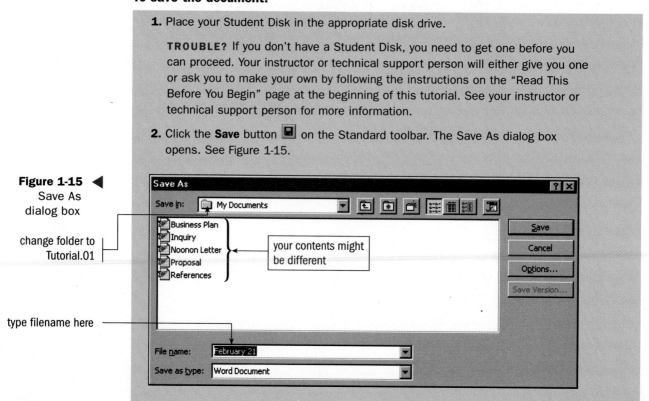

your contents might
be different

3. Type **Tacoma Job Fair Letter** in the File name text box.

4. Click the **Save in** list arrow, click the drive containing your Student Disk, and then double-click the **Tutorial.01** folder. The Tutorial.01 folder is now open for saving the file. See Figure 1-16.

Figure 1-16 ◀
Save As dialog box with Tutorial.01 folder open

folder on Student Disk

filename

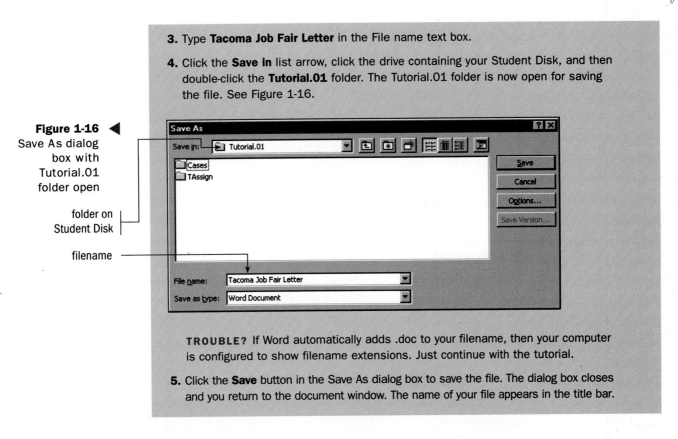

TROUBLE? If Word automatically adds .doc to your filename, then your computer is configured to show filename extensions. Just continue with the tutorial.

5. Click the **Save** button in the Save As dialog box to save the file. The dialog box closes and you return to the document window. The name of your file appears in the title bar.

Word Wrap

With your document saved, you're ready to complete Karen's letter. As you type the body of the letter, do not press the Enter key at the end of each line. When you type a word that extends into the right margin, both the insertion point and the word move automatically to the next line. This automatic text line breaking is called **word wrap**. You'll see how word wrap works as you type the body of Karen's letter.

To observe word wrap while typing a paragraph:

1. Make sure the insertion point is at Ln 20 Col 1 (according to the settings in the status bar). If it's not, move it to that location by pressing the arrow keys.

2. Type the following sentence slowly and watch when the insertion point automatically jumps to the next line: **Recently, you contacted our staff about the Chamber's decision to sponsor a job fair again this year.** Notice how Word automatically moves the last few words to a new line. See Figure 1-17.

Figure 1-17 ◀
Word wrapping text

beginning of first paragraph

word wrapped to new line

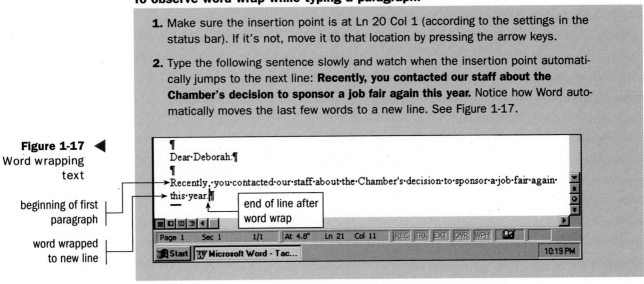

TROUBLE? If your screen does not match Figure 1-17 exactly, don't be concerned. The word or letter at which word wrap occurred in your document and the status bar values might be different from Figure 1-17 because fonts have varying letter widths and produce slightly different measurements on monitors. Continue with Step 3. If you see any other AutoText tips as you type, ignore them.

3. Press the **spacebar** twice, and type **We are interested in participating as we have done in the past.** (including the period) to enter the rest of the first paragraph of the letter.

4. Press the **Enter** key to end the first paragraph, and then press the **Enter** key again to double space between the first and second paragraphs.

Scrolling

After you finish the last set of steps, the insertion point will probably be at the bottom of your document window. It might seem that no room is left in the document window to type the rest of Karen's letter. However, as you continue to add text at the end of your document, the text that you typed earlier will scroll (or shift up) and disappear from the top of the document window. You'll see how scrolling works as you enter the final text of Karen's letter.

To observe scrolling while you're entering text:

1. Make sure the insertion point is at the bottom of the screen, to the left of the second paragraph mark in the body of the letter.

2. Type the second paragraph, as shown in Figure 1-18, and then press the **Enter** key twice to insert a blank line. Notice that as you type the paragraph, the top of the letter scrolls off the top of the document window. Don't worry if you make a mistake in your typing. You'll learn a number of ways to correct errors in the next section.

Figure 1-18 ◀
Text scrolled
off the screen

date and inside
address scrolled
off the screen

second paragraph

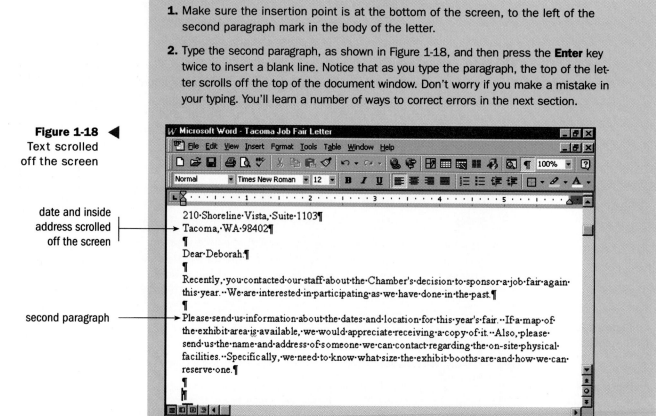

Correcting Errors

Have you made any typing mistakes yet? If so, don't worry. The advantage of using a word processor is that you can correct mistakes quickly and efficiently. Word provides several ways to correct errors when you're entering text.

Word

If you discover a typing error as soon as you make it, you can press the Backspace key to erase the characters and spaces to the left of the insertion point one at a time. Backspacing will erase both printing and nonprinting characters. After you erase the error, you can type the correct characters.

Word also provides a feature, called **AutoCorrect**, that checks for errors in your document as you type and automatically corrects common typing errors, such as "adn" for "and." If the spelling of a particular word doesn't appear as it would in the Word electronic dictionary or isn't in the dictionary (for example, a person's name), a wavy *red* line appears beneath the word. If you accidentally type an extra space between words or make a grammatical error (such as typing "he walk" instead of "he walks"), a wavy *green* line appears beneath the error. You'll see how AutoCorrect works when you intentionally make some typing errors.

To find common typing errors:

1. Carefully and slowly type the following sentence exactly as it is shown, including the spelling errors and the extra space between the last two words: **Word corects teh common typing misTakes you make.** Press the **Enter** key when you are finished typing. Notice that as you press the spacebar after the words "corects" and "misTakes," a wavy red line appears on the screen beneath each word, indicating that the word might be misspelled. Notice also that when you pressed the spacebar after the word "teh," Word automatically corrected the spelling to "the." After you pressed the Enter key, a wavy green line appeared under the last two words, alerting you to the extra space. See Figure 1-19.

Figure 1-19 ◄
Document
window
showing
typing errors

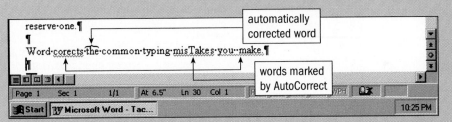

TROUBLE? If red and green wavy lines do not appear beneath mistakes, Word is probably not set to automatically check spelling and grammar as you type. Click Tools on the menu bar, and then click Options to open the Options dialog box. Click the Spelling and Grammar tab. Make sure there are check marks in the Check spelling as you type and the Check grammar as you type check boxes, and click OK. If Word does not automatically correct the incorrect spelling of "the," click Tools on the menu bar, click AutoCorrect, and make sure that all five boxes at the top of the AutoCorrect tab have check marks. Then scroll down the AutoCorrect list to make sure that there is an entry that changes "teh" to "the," and click OK.

TROUBLE? If the Office Assistant appears with a tip on correcting errors, you can close the Office Assistant window by clicking its Close button ✕.

2. Position the pointer I over the word "corects" and click the right mouse button. A list box appears with suggested spellings. See Figure 1-20.

Figure 1-20 ◄
List box
showing
AutoCorrect
suggested
spellings

click to replace
misspelled word

insertion point after
right-clicking
misspelled word

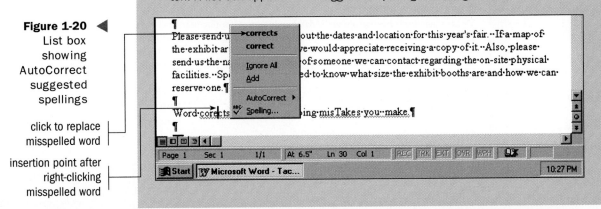

TROUBLE? If the list box doesn't appear, repeat Step 2 making sure you click the right mouse button, not the left one.

3. Click **corrects** in the list box. The list box disappears and the correct spelling appears in your document. Notice that the wavy red line disappears after you correct the error.

4. Position the pointer I directly over the word "misTakes" and click the right mouse button. A list box appears with suggested spellings.

5. Click **mistakes** in the list box. The list box disappears and the correct spelling appears in your document.

6. Press the → key until the insertion point is to the right of the letter "u" in the word "you." Press the **Delete** key to delete the extra space.

You can see how quick and easy it is to correct common typing errors with AutoCorrect. Use it or the Backspace or Delete keys now to correct mistakes you might have made when typing the first part of the letter. Before you continue typing Karen's letter, you'll need to delete your practice sentence.

To delete the practice sentence:

1. Click between the period and the paragraph mark at the end of the sentence.

2. Press and hold the **Backspace** key until the entire sentence is deleted. Then press the **Delete** key to delete the extra paragraph mark.

3. Make sure the insertion point is in line 29. There should be one nonprinting paragraph mark between the second paragraph and the paragraph you will type next.

Finishing the Letter

You're ready to complete the rest of the letter. As you type, you can use any of the techniques you learned in the previous section to correct mistakes.

To complete the letter:

1. Type the final paragraph of the body of the letter, as shown in Figure 1-21, and then press the **Enter** key twice. Accept or ignore AutoText tips as necessary. Your screen should look like Figure 1-21. Notice that the date and the inside address now scroll off the top of the document window.

Figure 1-21 ◀
Final paragraph

third paragraph ⟶

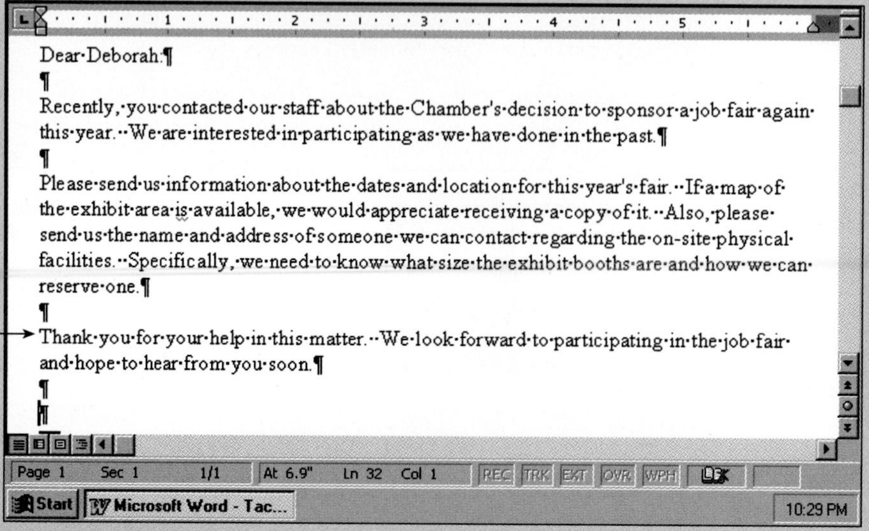

TROUBLE? If your screen does not match Figure 1-21 exactly, don't be concerned. Because of variations in font sizes and monitors, more or less text might have scrolled off your screen. Just continue with Step 2.

2. Type **Sincerely yours,** (including the comma) to enter the complimentary close.

3. Press the **Enter** key four times to allow space for Karen's signature.

4. Type **Karen Liu**, press the **Enter** key, and then type **Executive Director** to complete your letter. See Figure 1-22.

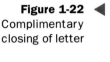

Figure 1-22
Complimentary
closing of letter

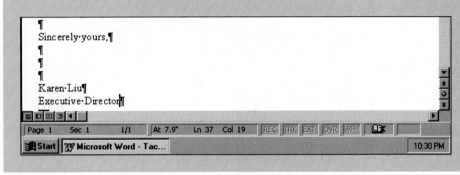

In the last set of steps, you watched the text at the top of your document move off your screen. You can scroll this hidden text back into view so you can read the beginning of the letter. When you do, the text at the bottom of the screen will scroll out of view.

To scroll the text using the scroll bar:

1. Position the mouse pointer ⫘ on the up arrow on the vertical scroll bar. Press and hold the mouse button to scroll the text. When the text stops scrolling, you have reached the top of the document and can see the beginning of the letter.

Now that you have completed the letter, you'll save the completed document.

Saving the Completed Letter

Although you saved the letter earlier, the text that you typed since then exists only in the computer's memory. That means you need to save your document again. It's especially important to save your document before printing. Then, if you experience problems that cause your computer to stop working while you are printing, you will still have a copy of the document containing your most recent additions and changes on your disk.

To save the completed letter:

1. Make sure your Student Disk is still in the appropriate disk drive.

2. Click the **Save** button 🖫 on the Standard toolbar. Because you named and saved this file earlier, you can save the document without being prompted for information. Word saves your letter with the same name you gave it earlier.

Previewing and Printing a Document

The current document window displays the text, but you cannot see an entire page without scrolling. To see how the page will look when printed, you need to use the Print Preview window.

To preview the document:

1. Click the **Print Preview** button 🔍 on the Standard toolbar. The Print Preview window opens and displays a full-page version of your letter, as shown in Figure 1-23. This shows how the letter will fit on the printed page.

Figure 1-23 ◀
Print preview
version of
the letter

one page button ──────

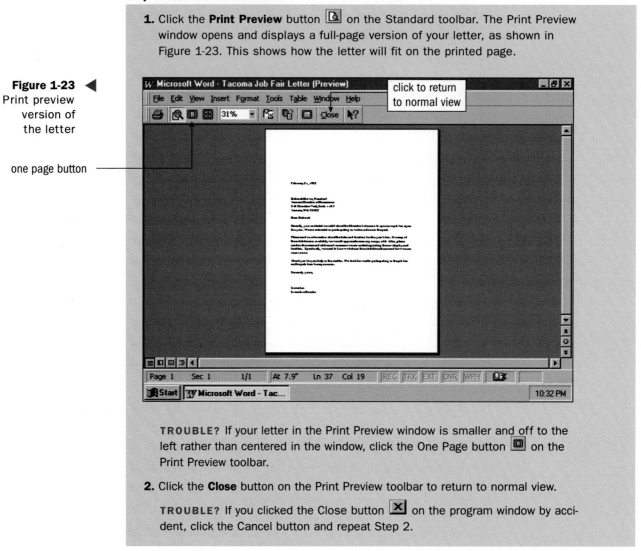

TROUBLE? If your letter in the Print Preview window is smaller and off to the left rather than centered in the window, click the One Page button 🔲 on the Print Preview toolbar.

2. Click the **Close** button on the Print Preview toolbar to return to normal view.

TROUBLE? If you clicked the Close button ☒ on the program window by accident, click the Cancel button and repeat Step 2.

You've seen how the letter will appear on the printed page. The text looks well-spaced and the letterhead will fit at the top of the page. You're ready to print the letter.

In each session, the first time you print from a shared computer, you should check the settings in the Print dialog box and make sure the number of copies is set to one. After that, you can *use* the Print button on the Standard toolbar to send your document directly to the printer without displaying the Print dialog box.

To print a document:

1. Make sure your printer is turned on and paper is in the printer.

2. Click **File** on the menu bar, and then click **Print**. The Print dialog box opens. See Figure 1-24.

Figure 1-24 ◄
Print dialog box

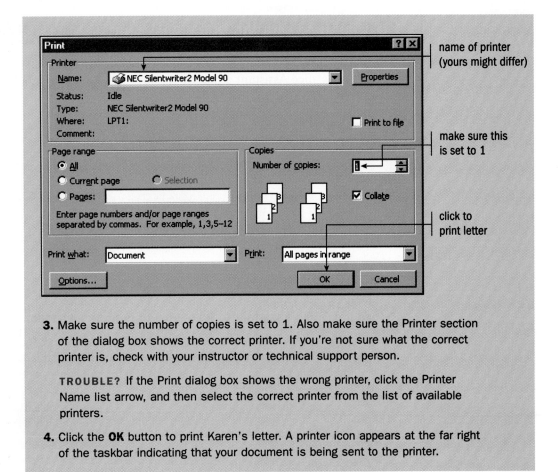

name of printer
(yours might differ)

make sure this
is set to 1

click to
print letter

3. Make sure the number of copies is set to 1. Also make sure the Printer section of the dialog box shows the correct printer. If you're not sure what the correct printer is, check with your instructor or technical support person.

   TROUBLE? If the Print dialog box shows the wrong printer, click the Printer Name list arrow, and then select the correct printer from the list of available printers.

4. Click the **OK** button to print Karen's letter. A printer icon appears at the far right of the taskbar indicating that your document is being sent to the printer.

Your printed letter should look similar to Figure 1-9 only without the Crossroads letterhead. The word wraps, or line breaks, might not appear in the same places on your letter because the size and spacing of characters vary slightly from one printer to the next.

Karen also needs an envelope to mail her letter in. Printing an envelope is an easy task in Word. You'll have a chance to try it in the Tutorial Assignments at the end of this tutorial. If you wanted to learn how to print an envelope yourself, you could use the Word Help system, which you'll learn about in the next section.

Getting Help

The Word Help system provides quick access to information about commands, features, and screen elements. The Contents and Index command on the Help menu displays the Help Topics window, which offers several options. You can look up a specific entry on the Index tab, search by general topics on the Contents tab, or search for information on a specific topic using the Find tab.

The What's This? command on the Help menu provides context-sensitive Help information. When you choose this command, the pointer changes to the Help pointer ▯?, which you can then use to click any object or option on the screen to see a description of the object.

You've already encountered another form of help, the Office Assistant, an animated figure that automatically offers advice on current tasks. You'll learn how to use the Office Assistant in the next section.

Getting Help with the Office Assistant

The **Office Assistant** is an interactive guide to finding information on the Help system. You can ask the Office Assistant a question, and it will look through the Help system to find an answer.

REFERENCE window	**USING THE OFFICE ASSISTANT**
	■ Click the Office Assistant button on the Standard toolbar (or choose Microsoft Word Help from the Help menu). ■ Type your question and then click the Search button. ■ Click a topic from the list of topics displayed. ■ To hide the Office Assistant, click its Close button.

You'll use the Office Assistant now to learn how to print an envelope.

To use the Office Assistant to learn how to print an envelope:

1. Click the **Office Assistant** button 🔲 on the Standard toolbar. The Office Assistant opens, offering help on topics related to the task you most recently performed (if any), and asking what you'd like to do. See Figure 1-25.

Figure 1-25 ◄
Office
Assistant

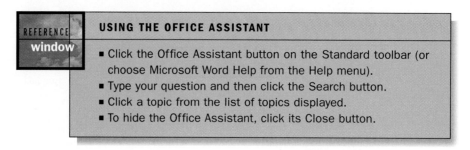

your options might be
in a different order

Office Assistant suggests topics
related to printing because you
just printed a document

type your
question here

don't worry if you see a
different animated figure

your Office Assistant might
display a lightbulb, indicating
a tip is available

2. Type **How do I print an envelope?** and then click the **Search** button.

3. Another dialog box opens, with more specific print topics. Click the **Print an address on an envelope** button to display information on that topic. See Figure 1-26.

Word

Figure 1-26 ◄
Help window on
printing an
envelope

click for more
information about
printing an envelope

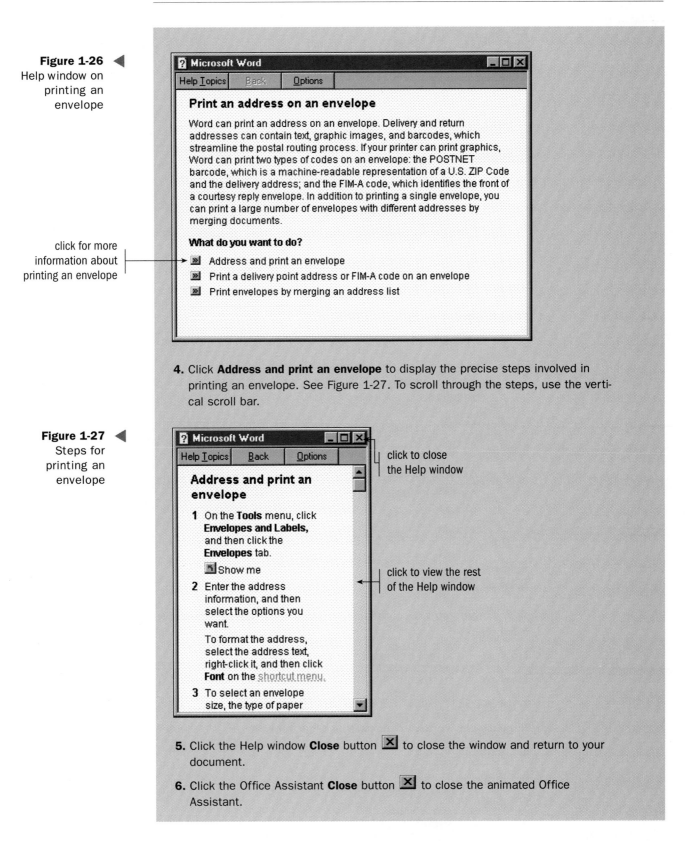

4. Click **Address and print an envelope** to display the precise steps involved in printing an envelope. See Figure 1-27. To scroll through the steps, use the vertical scroll bar.

Figure 1-27 ◄
Steps for
printing an
envelope

click to close
the Help window

click to view the rest
of the Help window

5. Click the Help window **Close** button ☒ to close the window and return to your document.

6. Click the Office Assistant **Close** button ☒ to close the animated Office Assistant.

Some Help windows have different formats than those you've just seen. However, they all provide the information you need to complete any task in Word.

Exiting Word

You have now finished typing and printing the letter to the Tacoma Chamber of Commerce, and you are ready to **exit**, or quit, Word to close the program.

REFERENCE window

EXITING WORD

- Click the Close button in the upper-right corner of the Word window (or click File on the menu bar, and then click Exit).
- If you're prompted to save changes to the document, click the Yes button; then, if necessary, type a name of the document and click the OK button.

Because you've completed the first draft of Karen's letter, you can close the document window and exit Word now.

To exit Word:

1. Click the **Close** button ⊠ on the document window to close the letter.

TROUBLE? If you see a dialog box with the message "Do you want to save changes to Tacoma Job Fair Letter?", you have made changes to the document since the last time you saved it. Click the Yes button to save the current version and close it.

2. Click the **Close** button ⊠ in the upper-right corner of the Word window. Word closes and you return to the Windows 95 desktop.

TROUBLE? If you see a dialog box with the message "Do you want to save changes to Document1?", click the No button.

You give the letter for the Tacoma Chamber of Commerce to Karen for her to review.

Quick Check

1 Why should you save a document to your disk several times, even if you haven't finished typing it?

2 How do you save a document for the first time?

3 How do you see the portion of the document that has scrolled from sight?

4 What is Print Preview and when should you use it?

5 In your own words, define each of the following:

a. scrolling

b. word wrap

c. AutoCorrect

d. Office Assistant

6 How do you exit Word?

Now that you have created and saved Karen's letter, you are ready to learn about editing and formatting a document in the next tutorial.

Tutorial Assignments

Karen received a response from the Chamber of Commerce containing the information she requested about the job fair, and Crossroads has firmed up its plans to participate as exhibitors. Karen now needs to staff the booth with Crossroads employees for each day of the five-day fair. She sends a memo to employees asking them to commit to a date. Create the memo shown in Figure 1-28 by completing the following:

1. If necessary, start Word and make sure your Student Disk is in the appropriate disk drive, and check your screen to make sure your settings match those in the tutorials.

2. Click the New button on the Standard toolbar to display a new, blank document.

3. Press the Caps Lock key and type "MEMORANDUM" (without the quotation marks) in capital letters and then press the Caps Lock key again.

4. Press the Enter key twice, type "Date:" (without the quotation marks), press the Tab key, and then insert today's date from your computer clock by clicking Insert on the menu bar, clicking Date and Time, and then clicking the date format that corresponds to February 21, 1998.

5. Continue typing the rest of the memo exactly as shown in Figure 1-28, including any misspellings and extra words. (This will give you a chance to practice correcting errors in Step 7.) Instead of Karen Liu's name after "From", however, type your own. Press the Tab key after "To:" "From:", and RE:" to align the memo heading evenly. If the Office Assistant appears, close it by clicking its Close button.

Figure 1-28 ◀
Sample memo

MEMORANDUM

Date: February 21, 1998

To: Staff Members

From: Karen Liu

RE: Dates for 1998 Job Fair

The the 1998 Job Fair sponsored by the Tacoma Chamber of Commerce will be held September 15-20 from 10:00 a.m. to 5:30 p.m.. This fiar provvides us with an oportunity to inform Tacoma residents about our services. In the past, we have each spent one day helping at the exhibit. Please let me know by tomorrow which day you would prefer this year.

Thanks.

6. Save your work as Fair Date Memo in the TAssign folder for Tutorial 1.

7. Correct the misspelled words, indicated by the wavy red lines. To ignore an AutoCorrect suggestion, click Ignore All. Then correct any grammatical or other errors indicated by wavy green lines. Use the Backspace key to delete any extra words.

8. Scroll to the beginning of the letter. Click at the beginning of the first line and insert room for the letterhead by pressing the Enter key until the first line is at about line 14.

9. Save your most recent changes.

10. Preview and print the memo.

11. Use the Office Assistant to find the steps necessary for printing an address on an envelope. On a piece of paper, write down the necessary steps.

EXPLORE

12. Print an envelope by following the steps you discovered in step 11. (Check with your instructor or technical support person to make sure you can print envelopes. If not, print on an 8½ × 11-inch sheet of paper.)

13. Close the document without saving your most recent changes.

14. Click the New button on the Standard toolbar to open a new, blank document.

EXPLORE

15. Write a letter to Deborah Brown at the Tacoma Chamber of Commerce, asking for information about food service at the job fair. Enter the date, the inside address, and the salutation as you did in the tutorial. Press the Enter key, and, when the Office Assistant opens, click the Get Help with writing the letter button. Following the Office Assistant's instructions, choose the desired options in the Letter Wizard dialog boxes. Click the Next button to move from one dialog box to the next. Type the text of your letter in the document window. Save the letter as Food Service in the TAssign folder for Tutorial 1, and print it.

EXPLORE

16. Use the What's This? feature to learn about the program's ability to count the words in your document. Click Help on the menu bar, and then click What's This? The mouse pointer changes to an arrow with a question mark. Click Tools on the menu bar, click Word Count, and then read the text box contents. When you are finished reading, click the text box to close it.

Case Problems

1. Letter to Confirm a Conference Date As convention director for the Tallahassee Convention and Visitors Bureau, you are responsible for promoting and scheduling the convention center. The Southern Georgia chapter of the National Purchasing Management Association has reserved the convention center for their annual conference on October 24–25, 1998 and has requested a written confirmation of their reservation.

Create the letter using the skills you learned in the tutorial. Remember to include today's date, the inside address, the salutation, the date of the reservation, the complimentary close, and your name and title. If the instructions show quotation marks around text you type, do not include the quotation marks in your letter. To complete the letter, do the following:

1. If necessary, start Word, make sure your Student Disk in the appropriate disk drive, and check your screen to make sure your settings match those in the tutorials.

2. Open a new blank page, and press the Enter key six times to insert enough space for a letterhead.

3. Use AutoText to type today's date at the insertion point.

4. Insert three blank lines after the date, and, using the proper business letter format, type the inside address: "Danetta Blackwelder, 618 Live Oak Plantation Road, Valdosta, GA 31355."

5. Insert a blank line after the inside address, type the salutation "Dear Ms. Blackwelder:", and then insert another blank line. If the Office Assistant appears click the Cancel button.

6. Write one paragraph confirming the reservation for October 24–25, 1998.

7. Insert a blank line and type the complimentary close "Sincerely," (include the comma).

8. Add four blank lines to leave room for the signature, and then type your name and title.

9. Use Word's Contents and Index command on the Help menu to find out how to center a line of text. Then center your name and title.

10. Save the letter as Confirmation Letter in the Cases folder for Tutorial 1.

11. Reread your letter carefully and correct any errors.

12. Save any new changes.

13. Preview the letter using the Print Preview button on the Standard toolbar.

14. Print the letter.

15. Close the document.

2. Letter to Request Information About a "Learning to Fly" Franchise You are the manager of the UpTown Sports Mall and are interested in obtaining a franchise for "Learning to Fly," a free-fall bungee jumping venture marketed by Ultimate Sports, Inc. After reading an advertisement for the franchise, you decide to write for more information.
Create the letter by doing the following:

1. If necessary, start Word, make sure your Student Disk in the appropriate disk drive, and check your screen to make sure your settings match those in the tutorials.

2. Open a new, blank document, and press the Enter key six times to insert sufficient space for a letterhead.

3. Use AutoText to type today's date at the insertion point.

4. Insert three blank lines after the date, and, using the proper business letter format, type the inside address: "Ultimate Sports, Inc., 4161 Comanche Drive, Colorado Springs, CO 80906."

5. Insert a blank line after the inside address, type the salutation "Dear Franchise Representative:", and then insert another blank line. Close the Office Assistant if necessary.

6. Type the first paragraph as follows: "I'm interested in learning more about the Learning to Fly bungee jumping franchise. As manager of UpTown Sports Mall, I've had success with similar programs, including both rock climbing and snowboarding franchises."(Do not include the quotation marks.)

7. Save your work as Bungee Request Letter in the Cases folder for Tutorial 1.

8. Insert one blank line, and type the following: "Please answer the following questions:". Then press the Enter key and type these questions on separate lines: "How much does your franchise cost?" "Does the price include the cost for installing the 70-foot tower illustrated in your advertisement?" "Does the price include the cost for purchasing the ropes and harnesses?" Then use the Office Assistant to find out how to add bullets, and, following its instructions, insert a bullet in front of each question.

9. Correct any typing errors indicated by wavy lines. (*Hint:* Because "bungee" is spelled correctly, click Ignore All on the AutoCorrect menu to remove the red line under "bungee.")

10. Insert another blank line, and type the complimentary close "Sincerely," (include the comma).

11. Insert three blank lines to leave room for the signature, and type your full name and title. Then press the Enter key and type "UpTown Sports Mall."

12. Save the letter with changes.

13. Preview the letter using the Print Preview button.

14. Print the letter.

15. Close the document.

3. Memo of Congratulations Glenna Zumbrennen is owner, founder, and president of Cuisine Unlimited. She was recently recognized as the 1998 New Hampshire Woman Business Owner of the Year by the National Association of Women Business Owners. She was also named to the 1998 Small Business Administration Advisory Council. Do the following:

1. If necessary, start Word, make sure your Student Disk in the appropriate disk drive, and check your screen to make sure your settings match those in the tutorials.

2. Write a brief memo congratulating Glenna on receiving these awards. Remember to use the four-part planning process. You should plan the content, organization, and style of the memo, and use a standard memo format similar to the one shown in Figure 1-28.

3. Save the document as Awards Memo in the Cases folder for Tutorial 1.

4. Preview the memo using the Print Preview button.

5. Print the memo.

6. Close the document.

4. Writing a Personal Letter with the Letter Template Word provides templates, which are models with predefined formatting, to help you create documents quickly and effectively. For example, the Letter template helps you create letters with professional-looking letterheads and with various letter formats. Do the following:

1. If necessary, start Word, make sure your Student Disk in the appropriate disk drive, and check your screen to make sure your settings match those in the tutorials.

2. Click File on the menu bar, and then click New. The New dialog box opens.

3. Click the Letters & Faxes tab, click Contemporary Letter, and then click the OK button.

4. Follow the instructions given in the document window. You might be asked to type personal information such as your name and address.

5. For the inside (recipient's) name and address, type a real or fictitious name and address.

6. In the body of the letter, include a sentence or two explaining that you're using the Word Letter template to create this letter.

7. After typing the letter, make sure that you're listed as the person sending the letter. (Someone else's name might be listed if you're not using your own computer or the personal information is already entered into Word.)

8. Save the letter as My Template Letter (in the Cases folder for Tutorial 1) and then print it.

9. If you completed Step 11 in the Tutorial Assignments, create an envelope for this letter and print it (if necessary, on an 8½ x 11 inch sheet of paper).

10. Close the document.

Lab Assignments

These Lab Assignments are designed to accompany the interactive Course Lab called Word Processing. To start the Word Processing Lab, click the Start button on the Windows 95 taskbar, point to Programs, point to Course Labs, point to New Perspectives Applications, and click Word Processing. If you do not see Course Labs on your Programs menu, see your instructor or technical support person.

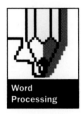

Word
Processing

Word Processing Word processing software is the most popular computerized productivity tool. In this Lab you will learn how word processing software works.

1. Click the Steps button to learn how word processing software works. As you proceed through the Steps, answer all of the Quick Check questions that appear. After you complete the Steps, you will see a Quick Check summary report. Follow the instructions on the screen to print this report.

2. Click the Explore button to begin. Click File on the menu bar, and then click Open to display the Open dialog box. Click the file TIMBER.TEX, and then press the Enter key to open the letter to Northern Timber Company. Make the following modifications to the letter, and then print it. You do not need to save the letter.
   a. In the first and last lines of the letter, change "Jason Kidder" to your name.
   b. Change the date to today's date.
   c. Select the second paragraph, which begins "Your proposal did not include. . ." Move this paragraph so it is the last paragraph in the text of the letter.
   d. Change the cost of a permanent bridge to $20,000.
   e. Spell check the letter.

3. Using Explore, open the file STARS.TEX. Make the following modifications to the document, and then print it. You do not need to save the document.
   a. Center and bold the title.
   b. Change the title font to 16 point Arial.
   c. Bold DATE, SHOWER, and LOCATION.
   d. Move the January 2–3 line to the top of the list.
   e. Number the items in the list 1., 2., 3., and so on.
   f. Add or delete tabs to realign the columns.
   g. Double space the entire document.

4. Using Explore, compose a one-page, double-spaced letter to your parents or to a friend. Make sure you date and spell check the letter. Print the letter and sign it. You do not need to save your letter.

Editing and Formatting a Document

Preparing an Annuity Plan Description for Right-Hand Solutions

CASE

Right-Hand Solutions

Reginald Thomson is a contract specialist for Right-Hand Solutions, a company that provides small businesses with financial and administrative services. Right-Hand Solutions contracts with independent insurance companies to prepare insurance plans and investment opportunities for these small businesses. Brandi Paxman, vice president of administrative services, asked Reginald to plan and write a document that describes the tax-deferred annuity plan for their clients' employee handbooks. Now that Brandi has commented on and corrected the draft, Reginald asks you to make the necessary changes and print the document.

In this tutorial, you will edit the annuity plan description according to Brandi's comments. You will open a draft of the annuity plan, resave it, and delete a phrase. You'll move text using two different methods, and find and replace one version of the company name with another.

You will also change the overall look of the document by changing margins, indenting and justifying paragraphs, and copying formatting from one paragraph to another. You'll create a bulleted list to emphasize the types of financial needs the annuity plan will cover and a numbered list for the conditions under which employees can receive funds. Then you'll make the title more prominent by centering it, changing its font, and enlarging it. You'll italicize the questions within the plan to set them off from the rest of the text, and underline an added note about how to get further information to give it emphasis. Finally, you will print a copy of the plan so you can proofread it.

SESSION

2.1

In this session you will edit Reginald's document by deleting words and by moving text within the document. Then you'll find and replace text throughout the document.

Opening the Document

Brandi's editing marks and notes on the first draft are shown in Figure 2-1. You'll begin by opening the first draft of the description, which has the filename Annuity.

Figure 2-1 ◄
Draft of annuity
plan showing
Brandi's edits
(page 1)

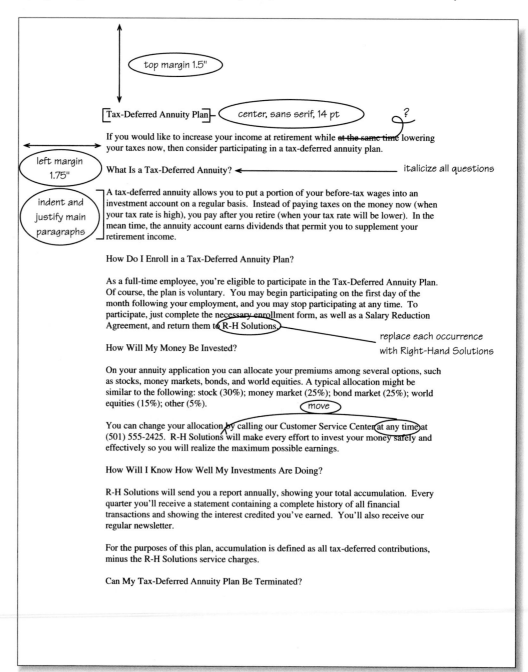

Figure 2-1 ◀
Draft of annuity
plan showing
Brandi's edits
(page 2)

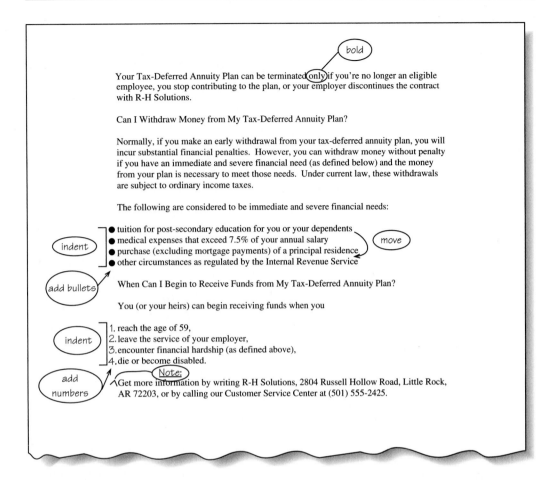

To open the document:

1. Place your Student Disk into the appropriate disk drive.

2. Start Word as usual.

3. Click the **Open** button 📂 on the Standard toolbar to display the Open dialog box, shown in Figure 2-2.

Figure 2-2 ◀
The open
document

names and files
specified here |

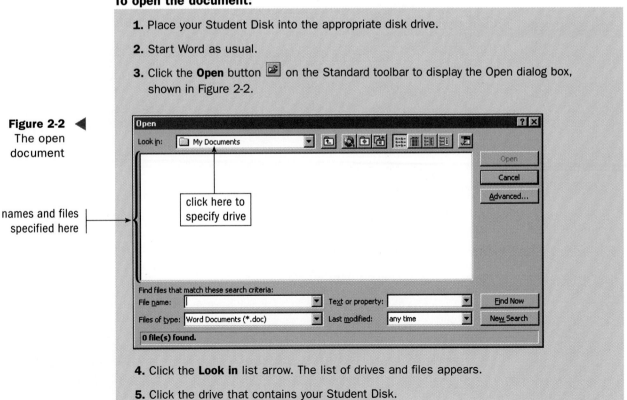

4. Click the **Look in** list arrow. The list of drives and files appears.

5. Click the drive that contains your Student Disk.

6. Double-click the **Tutorial.02** folder.

7. Click **Annuity** to select the file.

TROUBLE? If you see "Annuity.doc" in the folder, Windows 95 might be configured so that the filename extension is displayed. Click Annuity.doc and continue with Step 8. If you can't find the file with or without the filename extension, make sure you're looking in the Tutorial.02 folder and on the drive that contains your Student Disk, and check to make sure the Files of type text box displays Word Documents or All Files. If you still can't locate the file, ask your instructor or technical support person for help.

8. Click the **Open** button. The document opens, with the insertion point at the beginning of the document. See Figure 2-3.

Figure 2-3
The open document

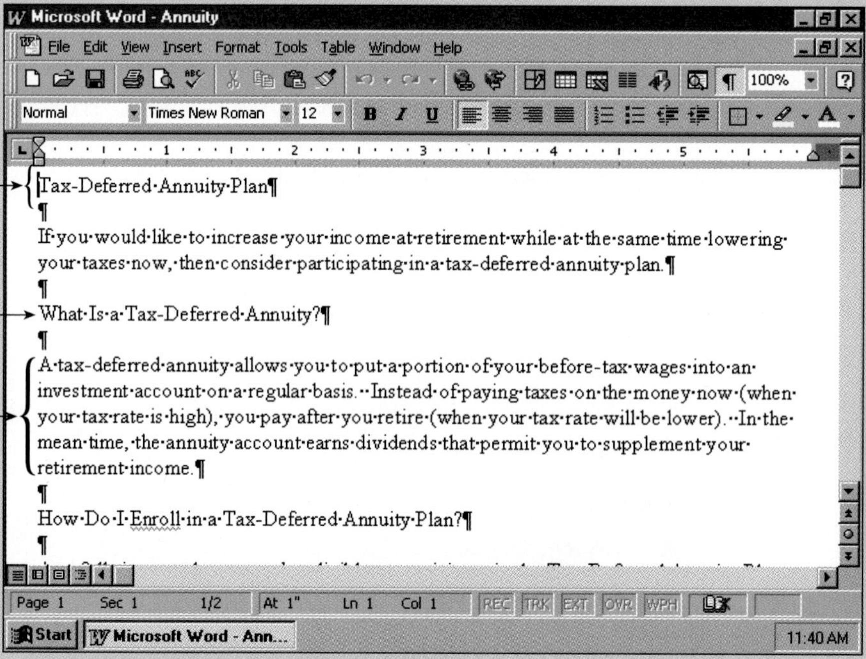

title

heading (question)

main paragraph (answer)

9. Check that your screen matches Figure 2-3. For this tutorial, display the nonprinting characters so that the formatting elements (tabs, paragraph marks, and so forth) are visible and easier to change.

Renaming the Document

To avoid altering the original file Annuity, you will save the document using the filename RHS Annuity Plan. Saving the document with another filename creates a copy of the file and leaves the original file unchanged in case you want to work through the tutorial again.

To save the document with a new name:

1. Click **File** on the menu bar, and then click **Save As**. The Save As dialog box opens with the current filename highlighted in the File name text box.

2. Click to the left of "Annuity" in the File name text box, type **RHS**, and then press the **spacebar**. Press the → key to move the insertion point to the right of the letter "y" in "Annuity," press the **spacebar**, and then type **Plan**. The filename changes to RHS Annuity Plan.

3. Click the **Save** button to save the document with the new filename.

Now you can edit the document. To make all of Brandi's edits, you'll need to learn how to quickly move the insertion point to any location in the document.

Moving the Insertion Point Around the Document

The arrow keys on your keyboard, ←, →, ↑, and ↓, allow you to move the insertion point one character at a time to the left or right, or one line at a time up or down. If you want to move more than one character or one line at a time, you can point and click in other parts of a line or the document. You can also press a combination of keys to move the insertion point. As you become more experienced with Word, you'll decide for yourself which method you prefer.

To see how quickly you can move through the document, you'll use keystrokes to move the insertion point to the beginning of the second page and to the end of the document.

To move the insertion point with keystrokes:

1. Press and hold down the **Ctrl** key while you press the **Page Down** key to move the insertion point to the beginning of the next page. Notice that the status bar indicates that the insertion point is now on page 2.

2. Press the ↑ key twice to move to the previous paragraph. Notice the automatic page break, a dotted line that Word inserts automatically to mark the beginning of the new page. See Figure 2-4. As you insert and delete text or change formatting in a document, the location of the automatic page breaks in your document continually adjust to account for the edits.

Figure 2-4 ◀
Automatic
page break

insertion point at
the end of page 1

automatic
page break

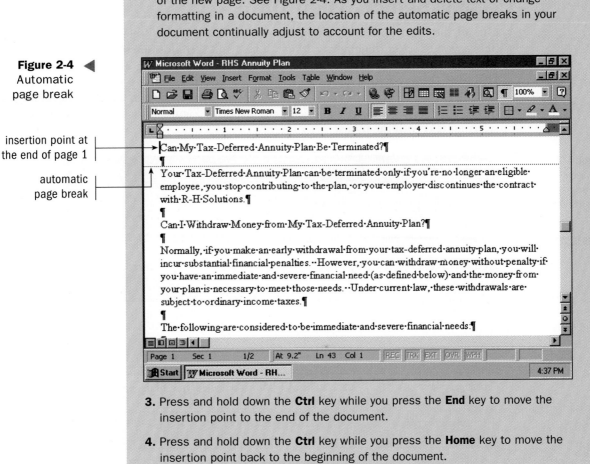

3. Press and hold down the **Ctrl** key while you press the **End** key to move the insertion point to the end of the document.

4. Press and hold down the **Ctrl** key while you press the **Home** key to move the insertion point back to the beginning of the document.

Figure 2-5 summarizes the keystrokes you can use to move the insertion point around the document.

Figure 2-5 ◀
Key strokes for
moving the
insertion point

Press	To Move Insertion Point
← or →	Left or right one character at a time
↑ or ↓	Up or down one line at a time
Ctrl + ← or Ctrl + →	Left or right one word at a time
Ctrl + ↑ or Ctrl + ↓	Up or down one paragraph at a time
Home or End	To the beginning or to the end of the current line
Ctrl + Home or Ctrl + End	To the beginning or to the end of the document
PageUp or PageDown	To the previous screen or to the next screen
Alt + Ctrl + PageUp or Alt + Ctrl + PageDown	To the top or to the bottom of the document window
Ctrl + PageUp or Ctrl + PageDown	To the beginning of the previous page or the next page

Using Select, Then Do

One of the most powerful editing features in Word is the "select, then do" feature. It allows you to select (highlight) a block of text and then do something to that text such as deleting, moving, or formatting it. You can select text using either the mouse or the keyboard; however, the mouse is usually the easier and more efficient way. You can quickly select a line or paragraph by clicking on the **selection bar**, which is the blank space in the left margin area of the document window. Figure 2-6 summarizes methods for selecting text with the mouse.

Figure 2-6 ◀
Methods for
selecting text
with the mouse

To Select	Do This
A word	Double-click the word
A line	Click in the selection bar next to the line
A sentence	Press and hold down the Ctrl key and click within the sentence
Multiple lines	Click and drag in the selection bar next to the lines
A paragraph	Double-click in the selection bar next to the paragraph, or triple-click within the paragraph
Multiple paragraphs	Click and drag in the selection bar next to the paragraphs, or triple-click and drag
The entire document	Press and hold down the Ctrl key and click in the selection bar, or triple-click in the selection bar
A block of text	Click at the beginning of a block, press and hold down the Shift key and click at the end of the block; highlights all the words in the block

Deleting Text

Brandi wants you to delete the phrase "at the same time" in the first paragraph of the document. You'll use the "select, then do" feature to delete the phrase now.

To select and delete a phrase from the text:

1. Click and drag I over the phrase "at the same time" located in the first line of the first paragraph. The phrase and the space following it are highlighted, as shown in Figure 2-7. Notice that dragging the pointer over the second and successive words automatically selects the entire words and the spaces following them. This makes it much easier to select words and phrases than selecting them one character at a time.

Figure 2-7 ◀
Phrase
selected
for deletion

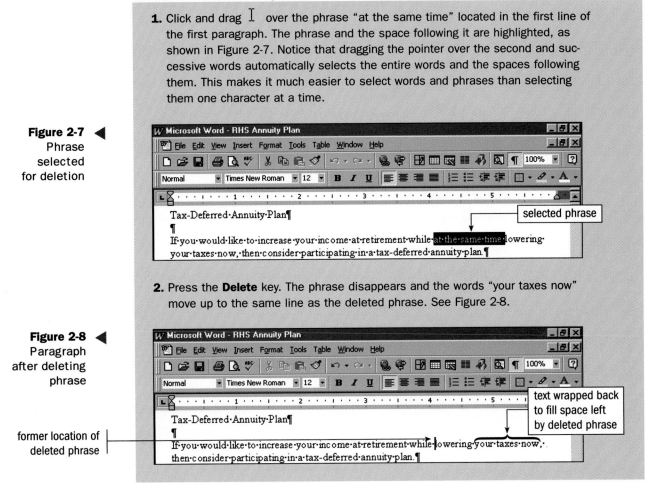

2. Press the **Delete** key. The phrase disappears and the words "your taxes now" move up to the same line as the deleted phrase. See Figure 2-8.

Figure 2-8 ◀
Paragraph
after deleting
phrase

former location of
deleted phrase

After rereading the paragraph, Reginald decides the phrase shouldn't have been deleted after all. He checks with Brandi and she agrees. You could retype the text, but there's an easier way to restore the phrase.

Using the Undo and Redo Commands

To undo (or reverse) the very last thing you did, simply click the Undo button on the Standard toolbar. If you want to reinstate your original change, the Redo button reverses the action of the Undo button (or redoes the undo). To undo anything more than your last action, you can click the Undo list arrow on the Standard toolbar. This list shows your most recent actions. Undo reverses the action only at its original location. You can't delete a word or phrase and then undo it at a different location.

REFERENCE window

USING UNDO AND REDO

- Click the Undo button on the Standard toolbar (or click Edit on the menu bar, and then click Undo) to reverse the very last thing you did.
- To reverse several previous actions, click the Undo list arrow on the Standard toolbar. Click an action on the list to reverse all actions up to and including the one you click.
- To undo your previous actions one-by-one, in the reverse order in which you performed them, click the Undo button one time for every action you want to reverse.
- If you undo an action by mistake, click the Redo button on the Standard toolbar (or click Edit on the menu bar, and then click Repeat) to reverse the undo.

Reginald suggested that you reverse your previous deletion, but left the final decision up to you. You decide to make the change to see how the sentence reads. Rather than retyping the phrase, you will reverse the edit using the Undo button.

To undo the deletion:

1. Click the **Undo** button [icon] on the Standard toolbar to undo your deletion. The phrase "at the same time" reappears in your document and is highlighted.

   TROUBLE? If the phrase doesn't reappear in your document and something else changes in your document, you probably made another edit or change to the document (such as pressing the Backspace key) between the deletion and the undo. Click the Undo button on the Standard toolbar until the phrase reappears in your document.

2. Click within the paragraph to deselect the phrase.

   As you read the sentence, you decide that it reads better without the phrase. Instead of selecting and deleting it again, you'll redo the undo.

3. Click the **Redo** button [icon] on the Standard toolbar.

   The phrase "at the same time" disappears from your document again.

4. Click the **Save** button [icon] on the Standard toolbar to save your changes to the document.

You have edited the document by deleting the text that Brandi marked for deletion. Now you are ready to make the rest of the edits she suggested.

Moving Text Within a Document

One of the most important uses of "select, then do" is moving text. For example, Brandi wants to reorder the four points Reginald made in the section "Can I Withdraw Money from My Tax-Deferred Annuity Plan?" on page 2 of his draft. You could reorder the list by deleting the sentence and then retyping it at the new location, but a much more efficient approach is to select and then move the sentence. Word has several ways to move text: drag and drop, cut and paste, and copy and paste.

Dragging and Dropping Text

The easiest way to move text within a document is called drag and drop. With **drag and drop,** you select the text you want to move, press and hold down the mouse button while you drag the pointer to a new location, and then release the mouse button.

Word

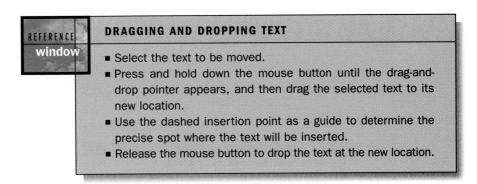

REFERENCE window

DRAGGING AND DROPPING TEXT

- Select the text to be moved.
- Press and hold down the mouse button until the drag-and-drop pointer appears, and then drag the selected text to its new location.
- Use the dashed insertion point as a guide to determine the precise spot where the text will be inserted.
- Release the mouse button to drop the text at the new location.

Brandi requested a change in the order of the items in the bulleted list on page 2 of Reginald's draft, so you'll use the drag-and-drop method to reorder the items. At the same time, you'll get some practice using the selection bar to highlight a line of text.

To move text using drag and drop:

1. Scroll through the document until you see "tuition for post-secondary education...", the first in the list of "immediate and severe financial needs:", which begins in the middle of page 2.

2. Click ⤴ in the selection bar to the left of the line beginning "tuition..." to select that line of text, including the return character. See Figure 2-9.

Figure 2-9 ◀
Selected text to drag and drop

pointer in selection bar

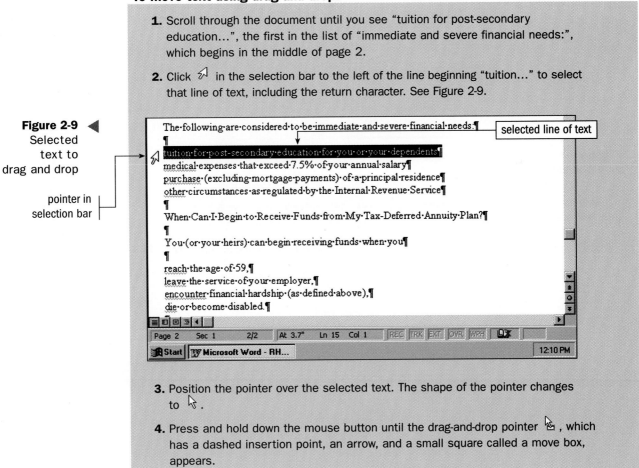

3. Position the pointer over the selected text. The shape of the pointer changes to ⤴ .

4. Press and hold down the mouse button until the drag-and-drop pointer ⤴ , which has a dashed insertion point, an arrow, and a small square called a move box, appears.

5. Drag the selected text down three lines until the dashed insertion point appears to the left of the word "other." Make sure you use the dashed insertion point to guide the text to its new location rather than the mouse pointer or the move box; the dashed insertion point marks the precise location of the drop. See Figure 2-10.

Figure 2-10 ◀
Moving text
with drag-and-
drop pointer

selected text
to be moved

dashed
insertion point

drag-and-drop pointer

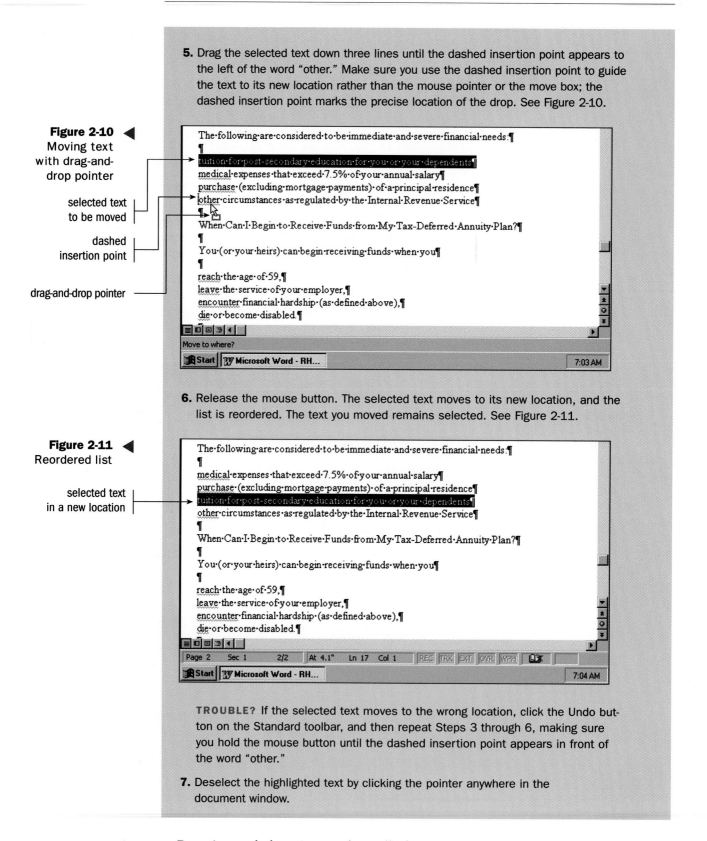

6. Release the mouse button. The selected text moves to its new location, and the list is reordered. The text you moved remains selected. See Figure 2-11.

Figure 2-11 ◀
Reordered list

selected text
in a new location

TROUBLE? If the selected text moves to the wrong location, click the Undo button on the Standard toolbar, and then repeat Steps 3 through 6, making sure you hold the mouse button until the dashed insertion point appears in front of the word "other."

7. Deselect the highlighted text by clicking the pointer anywhere in the document window.

Dragging and dropping works well if you're moving text a short distance in a document; however, Word provides another method, called cut and paste, that works well for moving text either a short distance or beyond the current screen.

Word

Cutting or Copying and Pasting Text

To **cut** means to remove text from the document and place it on the Windows Clipboard. The Clipboard stores only one item at a time; when you cut a new piece of text or a graphic, it replaces what was on the Clipboard. To **paste** means to transfer a copy of the text from the clipboard into the document at the insertion point. To perform a cut-and-paste operation, you select the text you want to move, cut (remove) it from the document, and then paste (restore) it into the document in a new location. If you don't want to remove the text from its original location, you can copy it (rather than cutting it) and then paste the copy in a new location. This procedure is known as "copy and paste."

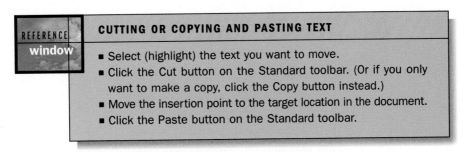

REFERENCE window	**CUTTING OR COPYING AND PASTING TEXT**
	■ Select (highlight) the text you want to move.
	■ Click the Cut button on the Standard toolbar. (Or if you only want to make a copy, click the Copy button instead.)
	■ Move the insertion point to the target location in the document.
	■ Click the Paste button on the Standard toolbar.

Brandi suggested moving the phrase "at any time" (in the paragraph beginning "You can change your allocation...") to a new location. You'll use cut and paste to move this phrase.

To move text using cut and paste:

1. Scroll the document up until you can see the paragraph just above the heading "How Will I Know...." on page 1.

2. Click and drag the mouse to highlight the complete phrase "at any time." See Figure 2-12.

Figure 2-12 ◄
Text to
move using
cut and paste

new location for text ⎯⎯⎯⎯⎯

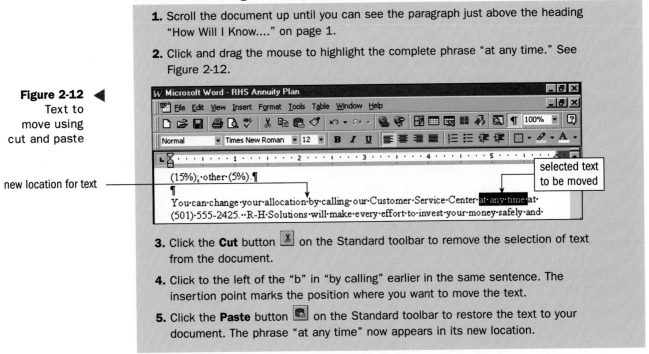

3. Click the **Cut** button [✂] on the Standard toolbar to remove the selection of text from the document.

4. Click to the left of the "b" in "by calling" earlier in the same sentence. The insertion point marks the position where you want to move the text.

5. Click the **Paste** button [📋] on the Standard toolbar to restore the text to your document. The phrase "at any time" now appears in its new location.

Keep in mind that you can also use the copy-and-paste method to move a copy of a block of text to another part of your document. Copy and paste works much the same way as cut and paste.

Finding and Replacing Text

When you're working with a longer document, the quickest and easiest way to locate a particular word or phrase is to use the Find command. If you want to replace characters or a phrase with something else, you can use the Replace command, which combines the Find command with a substitution feature. The Replace command searches through a document and substitutes the text you're searching for with the replacement text you specify. As Word performs the search, it will stop and highlight each occurrence of the search text and let you determine whether to substitute the replacement text by clicking the Replace button. If you want to substitute every occurrence of the search text with the replacement text, you can click the Replace All button.

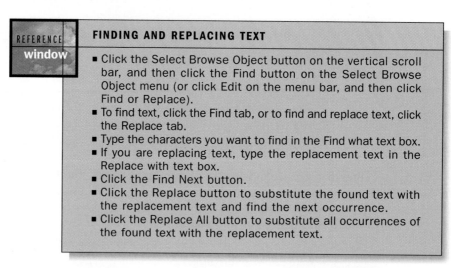

REFERENCE window

FINDING AND REPLACING TEXT

- Click the Select Browse Object button on the vertical scroll bar, and then click the Find button on the Select Browse Object menu (or click Edit on the menu bar, and then click Find or Replace).
- To find text, click the Find tab, or to find and replace text, click the Replace tab.
- Type the characters you want to find in the Find what text box.
- If you are replacing text, type the replacement text in the Replace with text box.
- Click the Find Next button.
- Click the Replace button to substitute the found text with the replacement text and find the next occurrence.
- Click the Replace All button to substitute all occurrences of the found text with the replacement text.

Brandi wants the shortened version of the company name, "R-H Solutions," to be spelled out as "Right-Hand Solutions" every time it appears in the text.

To replace "R-H Solutions" with "Right-Hand Solutions:

1. Click the **Select Browse Object** button ⊡ on the vertical scroll bar.

2. Click the **Find** button 🔍 on the Select Browse Object menu. The Find and Replace dialog box appears.

3. Click the **Replace** tab.

4. Type **R-H Solutions** in the Find what text box, press the **Tab** key, and type **Right-Hand Solutions** in the Replace with text box. See Figure 2-13.

Figure 2-13 ◀
Find and
Replace
dialog box

type search text here ——

type replacement
text here

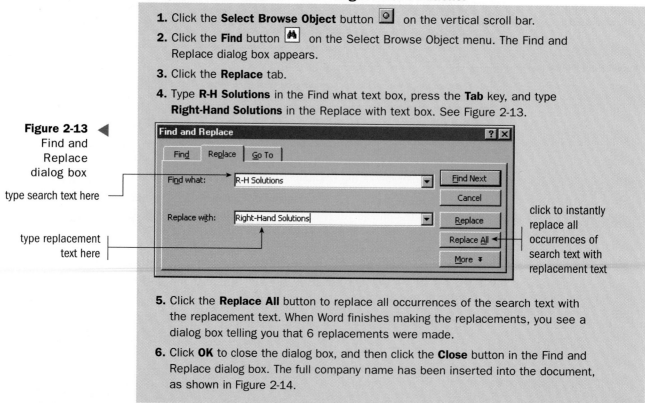

click to instantly
replace all
occurrences of
search text with
replacement text

5. Click the **Replace All** button to replace all occurrences of the search text with the replacement text. When Word finishes making the replacements, you see a dialog box telling you that 6 replacements were made.

6. Click **OK** to close the dialog box, and then click the **Close** button in the Find and Replace dialog box. The full company name has been inserted into the document, as shown in Figure 2-14.

Figure 2-14
The name
"Right-Hand
Solutions"
inserted into
the document

replacement text

replacement text

replacement text

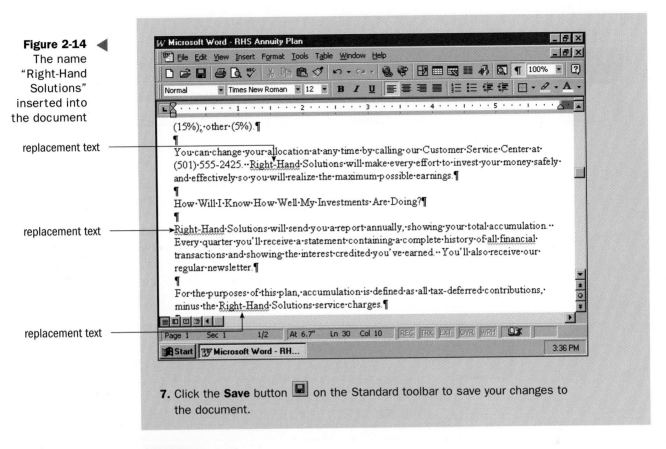

7. Click the **Save** button 🖫 on the Standard toolbar to save your changes to the document.

Quick Check

1. How do you open a document and save a copy of it with a new name?

2. Which key(s) do you press to move the insertion point to the following places:
   a. end of the document
   b. beginning of the document
   c. beginning of the next page

3. Explain how to delete text from a document.

4. Define the following terms in your own words:
   a. select, then do
   b. selection bar
   c. drag and drop

5. Explain how to select a phrase in the middle of a paragraph. Explain how to select a complete line of text.

6. What is the purpose of the Undo command? What is the purpose of the Redo command?

7. True or False: You can use the Undo command to restore deleted text at a new location in your document.

8. What is the difference between cut and paste, and copy and paste?

9. When you use the drag-and-drop method to move text, how do you know where the text will be positioned when it is dropped?

10. Explain how to find and replace text using the Select Browse Object button.

You have completed the content changes Brandi suggested, but she has some more changes for you that will improve the plan's appearance. In the next session, you'll enhance the Annuity Plan by changing the width, spacing, and alignment of text.

SESSION

2.2

In this session you will make the formatting changes Brandi suggested. You'll use a variety of formatting commands to change the margins, spacing, and tabs, and to justify and align the text. You'll also learn how to use the Format Painter, how to create bulleted and numbered lists, and how to change fonts, font sizes, and sizes.

Changing the Margins

In general, it's best to begin formatting by making the changes that affect the overall appearance of the document. In this case, you need to adjust the margin settings of the annuity plan summary.

Word uses default margins of 1.25 inches for the left and right margins, and 1 inch for the top and bottom margins. The numbers on the ruler (displayed below the Formatting toolbar) indicate the distance in inches from the left margin, not from the left edge of the paper. Unless you specify otherwise, changes you make to the margins will affect the entire document, not just the current paragraph or page.

REFERENCE window

CHANGING MARGINS FOR THE ENTIRE DOCUMENT

- With the insertion point anywhere in your document and no text selected, click File on the menu bar, then click Page Setup.
- If necessary, click the Margins tab to display the margin settings.
- Click the margins arrows to change each setting, or type a new margin value in each text box.
- Make sure the Apply to list box displays Whole document.
- Click the OK button.

You need to change the top margin to 1.5 inches and the left margin to 1.75 inches, as suggested by Brandi. The left margin needs to be wider than usual to allow space for making holes so that the document can be added to a three-ring binder. In the next set of steps, you'll change the margins with the Page Setup command. You can also change margins in page layout view; you'll practice that method in the Tutorial Assignments.

To change the margins in the annuity plan summary:

1. If you took a break after the last lesson, make sure Word is running, that the RHS Annuity Plan document is open, and that nonprinting characters are displayed.

2. Click once anywhere in the document to make sure no text is selected.

3. Click **File** on the menu bar, and then click **Page Setup** to open the Page Setup dialog box.

4. If necessary, click the **Margins** tab to display the margin settings. See Figure 2-15.

Word

Figure 2-15 ◀
Page Setup
dialog box

margins tab selected ——

text box ——

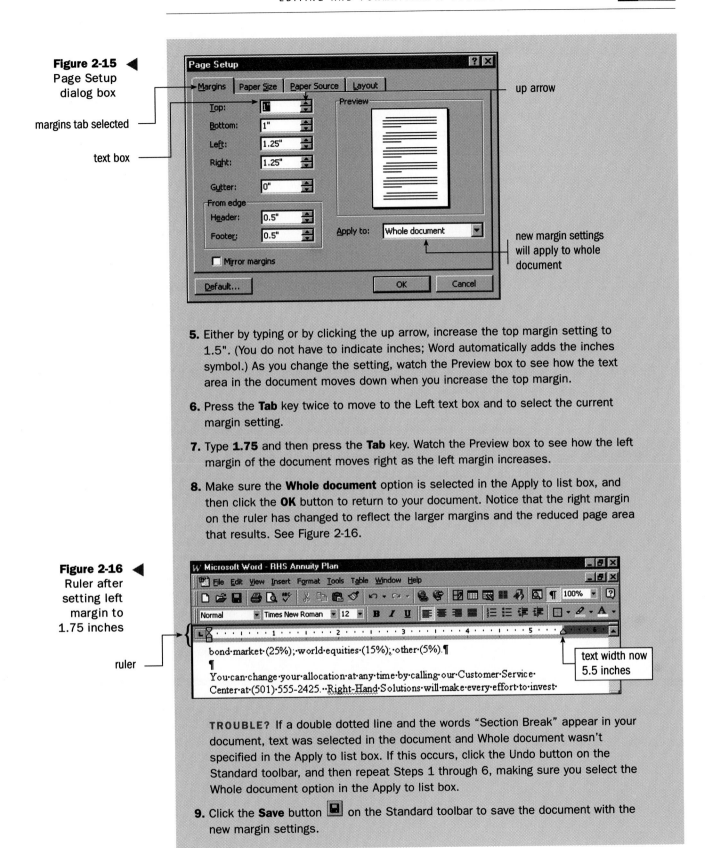

up arrow ——

new margin settings
will apply to whole
document

5. Either by typing or by clicking the up arrow, increase the top margin setting to 1.5". (You do not have to indicate inches; Word automatically adds the inches symbol.) As you change the setting, watch the Preview box to see how the text area in the document moves down when you increase the top margin.

6. Press the **Tab** key twice to move to the Left text box and to select the current margin setting.

7. Type **1.75** and then press the **Tab** key. Watch the Preview box to see how the left margin of the document moves right as the left margin increases.

8. Make sure the **Whole document** option is selected in the Apply to list box, and then click the **OK** button to return to your document. Notice that the right margin on the ruler has changed to reflect the larger margins and the reduced page area that results. See Figure 2-16.

Figure 2-16 ◀
Ruler after
setting left
margin to
1.75 inches

ruler ——

text width now
5.5 inches

TROUBLE? If a double dotted line and the words "Section Break" appear in your document, text was selected in the document and Whole document wasn't specified in the Apply to list box. If this occurs, click the Undo button on the Standard toolbar, and then repeat Steps 1 through 6, making sure you select the Whole document option in the Apply to list box.

9. Click the **Save** button 🖫 on the Standard toolbar to save the document with the new margin settings.

Now you are ready to make formatting changes that affect individual paragraphs.

Aligning Text

Word defines a paragraph as any text that ends with a paragraph mark symbol (¶). The alignment of a paragraph or document refers to how the text lines up horizontally between the margins. By default, text is aligned along the left margin but is ragged, or uneven, along the right margin. This is called **left alignment**. With **right alignment**, the text is aligned along the right margin and is ragged along the left margin. With **center alignment**, text is centered between the left and right margins. With **justified alignment**, full lines of text are spaced between or aligned along both the left and the right margins (similar to that in a newspaper column). The paragraph you are reading now is justified. The easiest way to apply alignment settings is by clicking buttons on the Formatting toolbar.

Brandi indicated that the title of the annuity plan description should be centered and that the main paragraphs should be justified. First, you'll center the title.

To center align the title:

1. Click anywhere in the title "Tax-Deferred Annuity Plan" at the beginning of the document.

2. Click the **Center** button ▤ on the Formatting toolbar. The text centers between the left and right margins. See Figure 2-17.

Figure 2-17 ◄
Title centered

centered title ——————

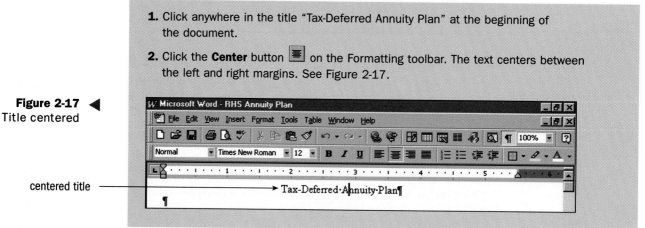

Now you'll use the Justify button to justify the text in the first two main paragraphs.

To justify the first two paragraphs using the Formatting toolbar:

1. Click anywhere in the first paragraph, which begins "If you would like to increase...", and click the Justify button ▤ on the Formatting toolbar. The justification would be easier to see if the paragraph had more lines of text. You'll see the effects more clearly after you justify the second paragraph in the document.

2. Move the insertion point to the second main paragraph, which begins "A tax-deferred annuity allows...".

3. Click ▤ again. The text is evenly spaced between the left and right margins. See Figure 2-18.

Figure 2-18 ◄
Text justified
using the
Formatting
toolbar

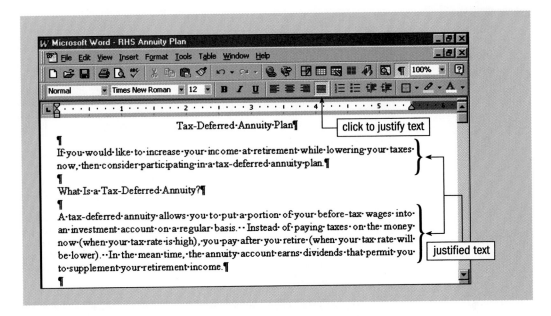

You'll justify the other paragraphs later. Now that you've learned how to change the paragraph alignment, you can turn your attention to indenting paragraphs.

Indenting a Paragraph

When you become a more experienced Word user, you might want to use some special forms of paragraph formatting, such as a hanging indent (where the first line of the paragraph extends into the left margin) or a right indent (where all lines of the paragraph are indented from the right margin). In this document, though, you'll only need to indent the main paragraphs 0.5 inches from the left margin. This is a simple kind of paragraph indent, requiring only a quick click on the Formatting toolbar's Increase Indent button. According to Brandi's notes, you need to indent all of the main paragraphs, starting with the second paragraph.

To indent a paragraph using the Increase Indent button:

1. Make sure the insertion point is still located anywhere within the second paragraph, which begins "A tax-deferred annuity allows...".

2. Click the **Increase Indent** button ⊞ on the Formatting toolbar twice. (Don't click the Decrease Indent button by mistake.) The entire paragraph moves right .5" each time you click the Increase Indent button. The paragraph is indented 1", .5" more than Brandi wants.

3. Click the **Decrease Indent** button ⊞ on the Formatting toolbar to move the paragraph left .5". The paragraph is now indented 0.5 inches from the left margin, as shown in Figure 2-19.

Figure 2-19
Indented
paragraph

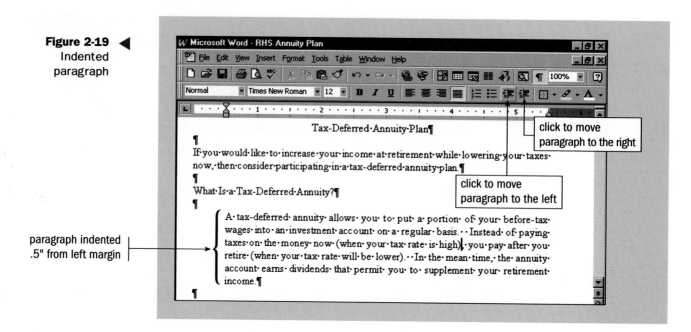

paragraph indented
.5" from left margin

You could continue to indent, and then justify, each paragraph individually, but there's an easier way—the Format Painter command. The Format Painter allows you to copy both the indentation and alignment changes to all the other main paragraphs in the document.

In addition to changing the horizontal alignment of text on the page, you can also change the vertical spacing, called **line spacing**. You can easily make the text double-spaced or, if you want the lines a little closer together, one-and-a-half spaced. You'll practice this in an Exploration Exercise in the Tutorial Assignment at the end of the tutorial.

Using Format Painter

The Format Painter makes it easy to copy all the formatting features of one paragraph to one or more other paragraphs. You'll use the Format Painter now to copy the formatting of the second paragraph to other main paragraphs. You'll begin by highlighting the paragraph whose format you want to copy. (Notice that you can't simply move the insertion point to that paragraph.)

To copy paragraph formatting with the Format Painter:

1. Double-click in the selection bar to select the second paragraph, which is indented and justified and begins "A tax-deferred annuity...".

2. Double-click the **Format Painter** button 🖋 on the Standard toolbar. Notice that the Format Painter button stays pressed. When you move the pointer over text it changes to 🔏 to indicate that the format of the selected paragraph can be painted (or copied) onto another paragraph.

3. Scroll down, and then click anywhere in the third paragraph, which begins "As a full-time employee...". The format of the third paragraph shifts to match the format of the selected paragraph. See Figure 2-20. As you can see, both paragraphs are now indented and justified. The pointer remains as the Format Painter pointer.

Word

Figure 2-20 ◀
Formats copied
with Format
Painter

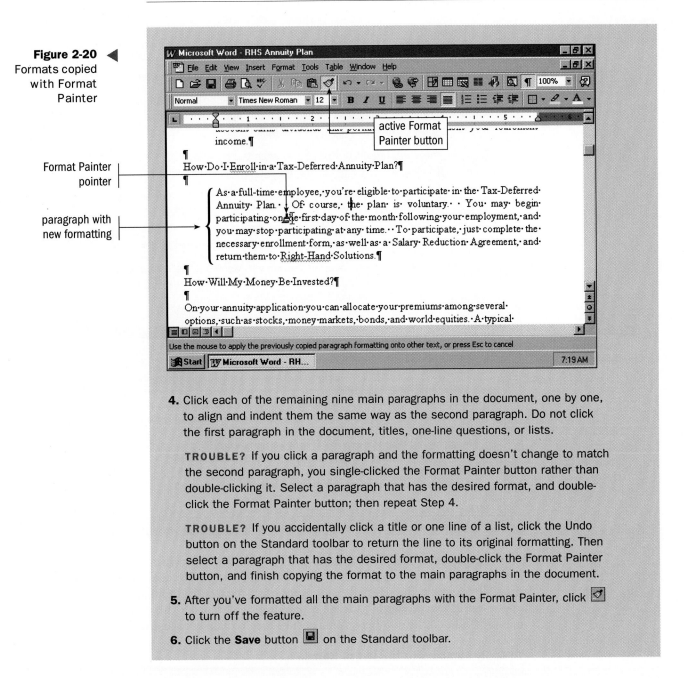

Format Painter
pointer

paragraph with
new formatting

4. Click each of the remaining nine main paragraphs in the document, one by one, to align and indent them the same way as the second paragraph. Do not click the first paragraph in the document, titles, one-line questions, or lists.

   TROUBLE? If you click a paragraph and the formatting doesn't change to match the second paragraph, you single-clicked the Format Painter button rather than double-clicking it. Select a paragraph that has the desired format, and double-click the Format Painter button; then repeat Step 4.

   TROUBLE? If you accidentally click a title or one line of a list, click the Undo button on the Standard toolbar to return the line to its original formatting. Then select a paragraph that has the desired format, double-click the Format Painter button, and finish copying the format to the main paragraphs in the document.

5. After you've formatted all the main paragraphs with the Format Painter, click [icon] to turn off the feature.

6. Click the **Save** button [icon] on the Standard toolbar.

All the main paragraphs in the document are formatted with the correct indentation and alignment. Your next job is to make the lists easier to read by adding bullets and numbers.

Adding Bullets and Numbers

Bullets (•) or numbers are useful whenever you need to emphasize a particular list of items. Brandi requested that you add bullets to the list of financial needs on page 2 to make them stand out.

To apply bullets to a list of items:

1. Scroll the document until you see the list of financial needs below the sentence "The following are considered to be immediate and severe financial needs:".

2. Select the four items that appear in the middle of page 2 (from "Medical expenses" to "Internal Revenue Service"). The text doesn't need to be fully highlighted; as long as you select a single character in a line, you can apply bullets to the paragraph.

3. Click the **Bullets** button on the Formatting toolbar to activate the Bullets feature. A rounded bullet, a special character, appears in front of each item, and each line indents to make room for the bullet.

4. Click the **Increase Indent** button to align the bullet text at the one-half inch mark, just below the left edge of the paragraphs above them.

TROUBLE? If the bullets in your document are already indented, you probably indented the list when you indented the main paragraphs earlier; don't click the Increase Indent button. If the bulleted list is now indented too much, click the Decrease Indent button until the bullet text is at the .5" mark on the ruler.

5. Click anywhere within the document window to deselect the text. Figure 2-21 shows the indented bulleted list. Note that the text itself, not the bullets, is indented.

Figure 2-21 ◀
Indented
bulleted list

bulleted list ────

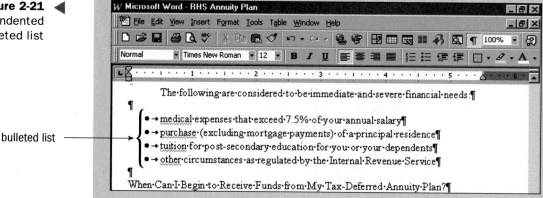

Next, you need to add numbers to the list that identifies when benefits can be received in the section below the bulleted list. For this you'll use the Numbering button, which automatically numbers the selected paragraphs with consecutive numbers and aligns them. If you insert a new paragraph, delete a paragraph, or reorder the paragraphs, Word automatically adjusts the numbers to make sure they remain consecutive.

To apply numbers to the list of items:

1. Scroll down to the next section, and then select the list that begins "Reach the age..." and ends with "...become disabled."

2. Click the **Increase Indent** button on the Formatting toolbar to indent the paragraph one-half inch. Notice that you can indent paragraphs before or after adding bullets or numbers. The order doesn't matter.

3. Click the **Numbering** button on the Formatting toolbar. Consecutive numbers appear in front of each item in the indented list.

4. Click anywhere in the document to deselect the text. Figure 2-22 shows the indented and numbered list.

Figure 2-22
Indented
numbered list

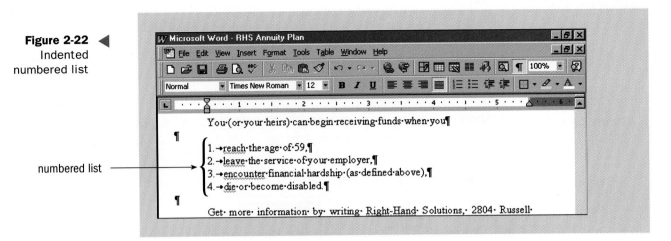

numbered list →

The text of the document is now properly aligned and indented. The bullets and numbers make the lists easy to read and give readers visual clues as to what type of information they contain. Next, you need to adjust the formatting of individual words.

Changing the Font and Font Size

All of Brandi's remaining changes have to do with changing fonts, adjusting font sizes, and emphasizing text with font styles. The first step is to change the font of the title from 12-point Times New Roman to a 14-point bold Arial. This will make the title stand out from the rest of the text.

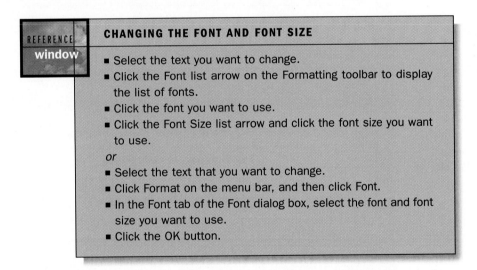

REFERENCE window

CHANGING THE FONT AND FONT SIZE

- Select the text you want to change.
- Click the Font list arrow on the Formatting toolbar to display the list of fonts.
- Click the font you want to use.
- Click the Font Size list arrow and click the font size you want to use.

or

- Select the text that you want to change.
- Click Format on the menu bar, and then click Font.
- In the Font tab of the Font dialog box, select the font and font size you want to use.
- Click the OK button.

Brandi wants you to change not only the font of the title, but also its size and style. To do this, you'll use the Formatting toolbar. She wants you to use a **sans serif** font, which is a font that does not have the small horizontal lines at the tops and bottoms of the letters. Sans serif fonts are often used in titles so they contrast with the body text. Times New Roman is a serif font, and Arial is a sans serif font. The text you are reading now is a serif font, and the text in the steps below is a sans serif font.

To change the attributes of the title using the Font command:

1. Press **Ctrl** + **Home** to move to the beginning of the document, and then select the title.

2. Click the **Font** list arrow on the Formatting toolbar. A list of available fonts appears in alphabetical order, with the name of the current font highlighted in the font list and in the Font text box. See Figure 2-23. Your list of fonts might be different from those shown in the figure. Fonts that have been used recently appear above the double line.

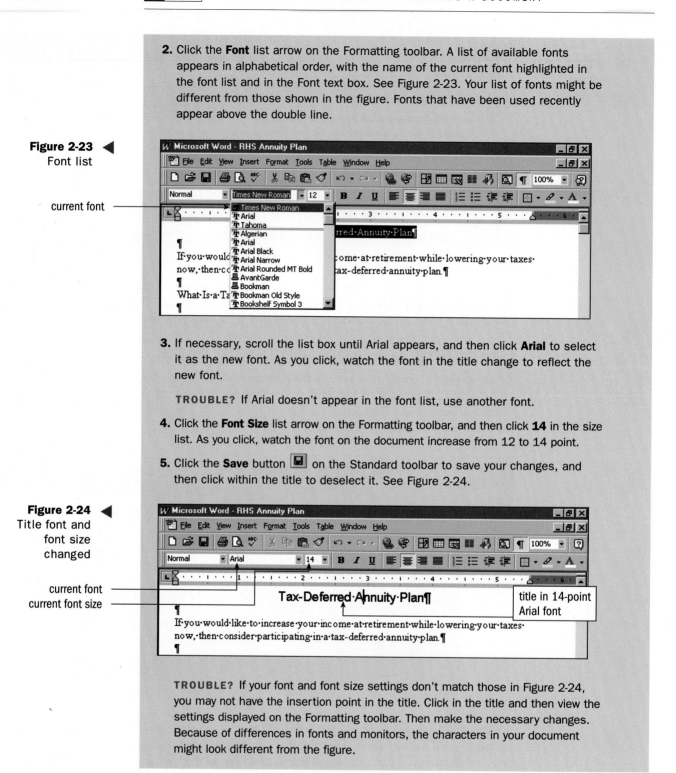

Figure 2-23 ◀
Font list

current font

3. If necessary, scroll the list box until Arial appears, and then click **Arial** to select it as the new font. As you click, watch the font in the title change to reflect the new font.

> **TROUBLE?** If Arial doesn't appear in the font list, use another font.

4. Click the **Font Size** list arrow on the Formatting toolbar, and then click **14** in the size list. As you click, watch the font on the document increase from 12 to 14 point.

5. Click the **Save** button 🖫 on the Standard toolbar to save your changes, and then click within the title to deselect it. See Figure 2-24.

Figure 2-24 ◀
Title font and
font size
changed

current font
current font size

title in 14-point
Arial font

Tax-Deferred·Annuity·Plan¶

> **TROUBLE?** If your font and font size settings don't match those in Figure 2-24, you may not have the insertion point in the title. Click in the title and then view the settings displayed on the Formatting toolbar. Then make the necessary changes. Because of differences in fonts and monitors, the characters in your document might look different from the figure.

Emphasizing Text with Boldface, Underlining, and Italics

You can emphasize words in your document with boldface, underlining, or italics. These styles help you make specific thoughts, ideas, words, or phrases stand out. Brandi marked a few words on Reginald's draft that need this kind of special emphasis.

Bolding Text

Brandi wants to make sure that clients' employees see that the tax-deferred annuity plan can be terminated only under certain conditions. You will do this by bolding the word "only."

To change the font style to boldface:

1. Scroll down so you can view the first line of the paragraph beneath the question "Can My Tax-Deferred Annuity Plan Be Terminated?" on page 2.

2. Select the word "only" (immediately after the word "terminated").

3. Click the **Bold** button ⬛ on the Formatting toolbar, and then click anywhere in the document to deselect the text. The word appears in bold, as shown in Figure 2-25.

Figure 2-25 ◄
Word in boldface

Bold button

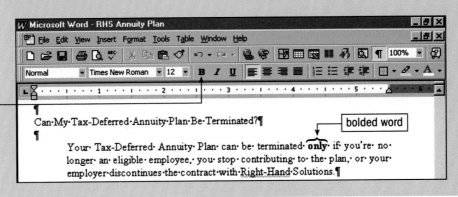

Underlining Text

The Underline command works in the same way as the Bold command. Brandi's edits indicate that the word "Note" should be inserted and underlined at the beginning of the final paragraph. You'll make both of these changes at once using the Underline command.

To underline text:

1. Press **Ctrl + End** to move the insertion point to the end of the document. Then move the insertion point to the left of the word "Get" in the first line of the final paragraph.

2. Click the **Underline** button ⬛ on the Formatting toolbar to turn on underlining. Notice that the Underline button remains pressed. Now, whatever text you type will be underlined on your screen and in your printed document.

3. Type **Note** and then click ⬛ to turn off underlining. Notice that the Underline button is no longer pressed, and the word "Note" is underlined.

4. Type : (a colon) and then press the **spacebar** twice. See Figure 2-26.

Figure 2-26 ◄
Word typed with underline

underlined word

Underline button

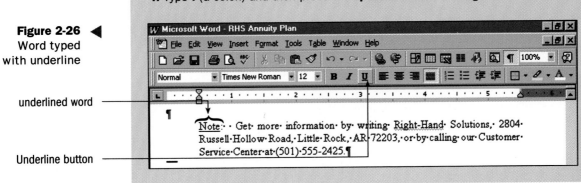

Italicizing Text

Next, you'll make annuity plan document conform with the other documents that Right-Hand Solutions produces by changing each question (heading) in the document to italics. This makes the document easier to read by clearly separating the sections. You'll begin with the first heading.

To italicize the question headings:

1. Press **Ctrl + Home** to return to the beginning of the document, and then select the text of the first heading, "What Is a Tax-Deferred Annuity?", by triple-clicking the text.

2. Click the **Italic** button *I* on the Formatting toolbar. The heading changes from regular to italic text.

3. Repeat Steps 1 and 2 to italicize the next heading. Now try a shorter way to italicize the text by repeating the formatting you just applied.

4. Select the next heading and then press the **F4** key. Repeat for each of the remaining five questions (headings) in the document. The italicized headings stand out from the rest of the text and help give the document a visual structure.

5. Click the **Save** button on the Standard toolbar to save your work.

You have made all the editing and formatting changes that Brandi requested for the annuity plan description. You are ready to print a copy of the document. You don't need to change any print settings, so you can use the Print button on the Standard toolbar.

To preview and print the document:

1. Click the **Print Preview** button on the Standard toolbar, and examine the document's appearance.

2. Click the **Print** button on the Print Preview toolbar. After a pause, the document prints.

3. Click the **Close** button on the Print Preview toolbar, then click the **Close** button ☒ on the program window to close your document and exit Word.

You now have a hard copy of the final annuity plan description, as shown in Figure 2-27.

Figure 2-27
Final version of
RHS annuity
plan (page 1)

Tax-Deferred Annuity Plan

If you would like to increase your income at retirement while lowering your taxes now, then consider participating in a tax-deferred annuity plan.

What Is a Tax-Deferred Annuity?

A tax-deferred annuity allows you to put a portion of your before-tax wages into an investment account on a regular basis. Instead of paying taxes on the money now (when your tax rate is high), you pay after you retire (when your tax rate will be lower). In the mean time, the annuity account earns dividends that permit you to supplement your retirement income.

How Do I Enroll in a Tax-Deferred Annuity Plan?

As a full-time employee, you're eligible to participate in the Tax-Deferred Annuity Plan. Of course, the plan is voluntary. You may begin participating on the first day of the month following your employment, and you may stop participating at any time. To participate, just complete the necessary enrollment form, as well as a Salary Reduction Agreement, and return them to Right-Hand Solutions.

How Will My Money Be Invested?

On your annuity application you can allocate your premiums among several options, such as stocks, money markets, bonds, and world equities. A typical allocation might be similar to the following: stock (30%); money market (25%); bond market (25%); world equities (15%); other (5%).

You can change your allocation at any time by calling our Customer Service Center at (501) 555-2425. Right-Hand Solutions will make every effort to invest your money safely and effectively so you will realize the maximum possible earnings.

How Will I Know How Well My Investments Are Doing?

Right-Hand Solutions will send you a report annually, showing your total accumulation. Every quarter you'll receive a statement containing a complete history of all financial transactions and showing the interest credited you've earned. You'll also receive our regular newsletter.

Word

Figure 2-27 ◀
Final version of
RHS annuity
plan (page 2)

For the purposes of this plan, accumulation is defined as all tax-deferred contributions, minus the Right-Hand Solutions service charges.

Can My Tax-Deferred Annuity Plan Be Terminated?

Your Tax-Deferred Annuity Plan can be terminated **only** if you're no longer an eligible employee, you stop contributing to the plan, or your employer discontinues the contract with Right-Hand Solutions.

Can I Withdraw Money from My Tax-Deferred Annuity Plan?

Normally, if you make an early withdrawal from your tax-deferred annuity plan, you will incur substantial financial penalties. However, you can withdraw money without penalty if you have an immediate and severe financial need (as defined below) and the money from your plan is necessary to meet those needs. Under current law, these withdrawals are subject to ordinary income taxes.

The following are considered to be immediate and severe financial needs:

- medical expenses that exceed 7.5% of your annual salary
- purchase (excluding mortgage payments) of a principal residence
- tuition for post-secondary education for you or your dependents
- other circumstances as regulated by the Internal Revenue Service

When Can I Begin to Receive Funds from My Tax-Deferred Annuity Plan?

You (or your heirs) can begin receiving funds when you

1. reach the age of 59,
2. leave the service of your employer,
3. encounter financial hardship (as defined above),
4. die or become disabled.

<u>Note</u>: Get more information by writing Right-Hand Solutions, 2804 Russell Hollow Road, Little Rock, AR 72203, or by calling our Customer Service Center at (501) 555-2425.

Quick Check

1. Name and describe the four types of text alignment or justification, and how to align and justify text using Word.

2. What is the purpose of the Format Painter and how does it work?

3. Explain how to indent a paragraph 0.5 inches or more from the left margin.

4. True or False: The larger the point size, the smaller the font that will be displayed and printed.

5 How do you apply bullets to a list of items?

6 Describe the steps necessary to bold a word or phrase.

7 Describe the steps necessary to change the font of a word or phrase.

8 Explain how to find the word "strategy" in a long document and replace every occurrence with the word "plan."

9 Explain how to change a document's margins.

In this tutorial, you have helped Reginald plan, edit, and format the annuity plan that will appear in the employee handbooks of Right-Hand Solutions' clients. Now that you have fine-tuned the content, adjusted the text appearance and alignment, and added a bulleted list and a numbered list, the plan is visually appealing and easy to read.

You give the hard copy to Reginald, who makes two photocopies—one for Brandi and one for the copy center, which copies and distributes the document to all clients of Right-Hand Solutions.

Tutorial Assignments

Now that Reginald has completed the description of the annuity plan, Brandi tells him that she also wants to include a sample quarterly statement and a sample contract change notice in the client's employee handbooks to show employees how easy the statements are to read. You'll open and format this document now.

1. If necessary, start Word, make sure your Student Disk is in the appropriate disk drive, and check your screen to make sure your settings match those in the tutorial.

2. Open the file RHSQuart from the TAssign folder for Tutorial 2 on your Student Disk, and save the document as RHS Quarterly Report.

3. Make all edits and formatting changes marked on Figure 2-28. However, when you substitute Right-Hand Solutions in place of We in the first paragraph, use copy and paste, copying the company name from the top of the letter (without the paragraph mark) before you bold it.

Figure 2-28 ◀

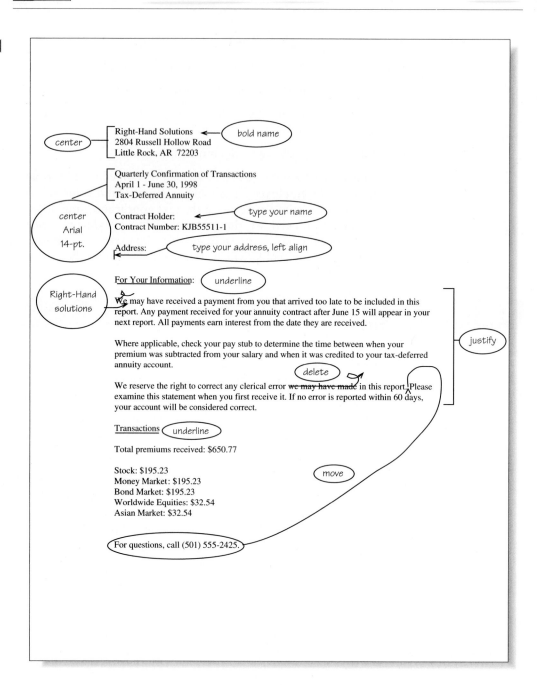

4. Save the document and print it.

5. Close the document.

6. Open the file RHSPort from the TAssign folder on your Student Disk, and save the file as RHS Portfolio Changes.

7. Make all the edits and formatting changes marked on Figure 2-29. However, instead of using the Formatting toolbar to change Current Allocation Accounts to bold 14 point, click Format on the menu bar, and then click Font to open the Font dialog box. Click the appropriate selections in the Font style and Size list boxes.

Figure 2-29 ◀

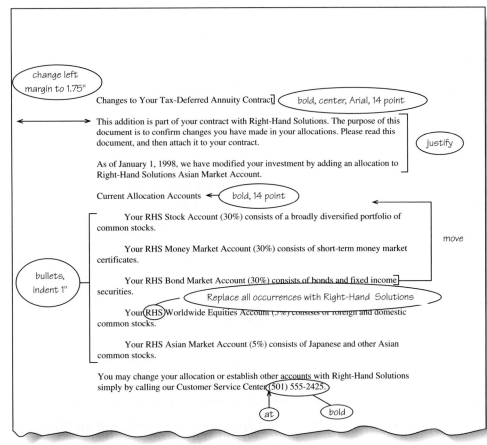

change left
margin to 1.75"

Changes to Your Tax-Deferred Annuity Contract   bold, center, Arial, 14 point

This addition is part of your contract with Right-Hand Solutions. The purpose of this
document is to confirm changes you have made in your allocations. Please read this
document, and then attach it to your contract.   justify

As of January 1, 1998, we have modified your investment by adding an allocation to
Right-Hand Solutions Asian Market Account.

Current Allocation Accounts   bold, 14 point

Your RHS Stock Account (30%) consists of a broadly diversified portfolio of
common stocks.

Your RHS Money Market Account (30%) consists of short-term money market
certificates.   move

bullets,
indent 1"   Your RHS Bond Market Account (30%) consists of bonds and fixed income
securities.

Replace all occurrences with Right-Hand Solutions

Your RHS Worldwide Equities Account (5%) consists of foreign and domestic
common stocks.

Your RHS Asian Market Account (5%) consists of Japanese and other Asian
common stocks.

You may change your allocation or establish other accounts with Right-Hand Solutions
simply by calling our Customer Service Center (501) 555-2425.

at   bold

 EXPLORE

8. Change the margins using the ruler in page layout view:
   a. Click the Page Layout View button.
   b. Select all the text in the document by pressing Ctrl + A.
   c. Position the pointer on the ruler at the right margin, which is indicated by a
      change from white to gray background, and then press and hold down the
      mouse button. The pointer changes to a two-headed arrow, which allows
      you to adjust the right margin. Drag the margin left to the 5" mark on the
      ruler, and then release the mouse button. Save the document.

 EXPLORE

9. Change the line spacing of the text.
   a. Make sure all the text in the document is selected.
   b. Click Format on the menu bar, and then click Paragraph to open the
      Paragraph dialog box.
   c. Click the Indents and Spacing tab.
   d. Click the Line spacing list arrow, and then click 1.5 lines.
   e. Click the OK button.

10. Click the Print Preview button on the Standard toolbar to check your work.

 **EXPLORE**

11. Use the Print command on the File menu to open the Print dialog box. Print
    two copies of the document by changing the Number of copies setting in the
    Print dialog box.

 EXPLORE

12. You can find out the number of words in your documents by using the Word
    Count command on the Tools menu. Use this command to determine the num-
    ber of words in the document, and then write that number in the upper-right
    corner of one of the printouts.

13. Save and close the document.

Case Problems

1. **Raleigh Rentals** Michele Stafford manages Raleigh Rentals, a storage facility in Huntsville, Alabama. She has written the draft of a tenant information sheet outlining Raleigh Rental's policies for new customers. She asks you to edit and format the document for her.

   1. If neccessary, start Word, make sure your Student Disk is in the appropriate disk drive, and check your screen to make sure your settings match those in the tutorials.

   2. Open the file Raleigh from the Tutorial 2 Cases folder on your Student Disk, and save it as Raleigh Rental Policies.

   3. Delete the word "general" from the first sentence of the first full paragraph. (Remember to use the Undo and Redo buttons to correct any editing mistakes as you work.)

   4. Delete the sentence at the end of the second paragraph that begins "If you renew your contract...".

   5. Insert the bolded sentence "A bill will not be sent to you." after the first sentence under the heading "Rental Payments".

   6. Delete the second paragraph under the heading "Rental Payments".

   7. Move the heading "Fees" and the sentence below it so that they appear after the "Rental Charges" section, not before it.

   8. Delete the phrase "not negotiable, and are" from the first sentence under the heading "Rental Charges".

   9. Change all of the margins (top, bottom, left, and right) to 1.5 inches.

   10. For each paragraph following a heading, indent the paragraph 0.5 inch and set the alignment to justify. (*Hint:* Format the first paragraph and then use the Format Painter to format each successive paragraph.)

   11. Use the Find tab in the Find and Replace dialog box to find the phrase "in writing" in the last sentence under the heading "Termination" and italicize it.

   12. Create bullets for the list under the heading "Delinquent Accounts," and indent the list 0.5 inch.

   13. Change both lines of the title to 16-point Arial (or another font of your choice).

   14. Center and bold both lines of the title.

   15. Bold all of the headings.

   16. Replace the misspelling "sub-let" with "sublet" wherever it appears in the document.

   17. Save, preview, and print the rental information sheet, and close the document.

2. **Synergy** Synergy provides productivity training for large companies across the country. Matt Patterson is Synergy's marketing director for the Northeast region. Matt wants to provide interested clients with a one-page summary of Synergy's productivity training.

   1. If neccessary, start Word, make sure your Student Disk is in the appropriate disk drive, and check your screen to make sure your settings match those in the tutorials.

   2. Open the file Synergy from the Tutorial 2 Cases folder on your Student Disk, and save it as Synergy Training Summary.

3. Change the title at the beginning of the document to a 14-point sans serif font. Be sure to pick a font that looks professional and is easy to read. (Remember to use the Undo and Redo buttons to correct any editing mistakes as you work.)

4. Center and bold the title.

5. Delete the word "main" from the second sentence of the first paragraph after the document title.

6. Create bullets for the list of training components following the first paragraph.

7. Under the heading "Personal Productivity Training Seminar" delete the second sentence from the first paragraph.

8. Under the heading "Personal Productivity Training Seminar" delete the phrase "in attendance at the seminar" from the first sentence in the second paragraph.

9. In the first paragraph under the heading "Management Productivity Training," move the second sentence beginning with "As a result" to the end of the paragraph.

10. Switch the order of the paragraphs under the "Field Services Technology and Training" heading.

11. Change the top margin to 1.5 inches.

12. Change the left margin to 1.75 inches.

13. Bold each of the headings.

14. Bold both occurrences of the word "free" in the second paragraph under the "Field Services Technology and Training" heading.

15. Save, preview, and print Synergy Training Summary, and then close the file.

3. **Rec-Tech** Ralph Dysktra is vice president of sales and marketing at Rec-Tech, an outdoor and sporting gear store in Conshohocken, Pennsylvania. Each quarter, Ralph and his staff mail a description of new products to Rec-Tech's regular customers. Ralph has asked you to edit and format the first few pages of this quarter's new products description.

1. If neccessary, start Word, make sure your Student Disk is in the appropriate disk drive, and check your screen to make sure your settings match those in the tutorials.

2. Open the file Backpack from the Tutorial 2 Cases folder on your Student Disk, and save it as Backpacker's Guide.

3. Delete the word "much" from the first sentence of the paragraph below the heading "Snuggle Up to These Prices". (Remember to use the Undo and Redo buttons to correct any editing mistakes as you work.)

4. Reverse the order of the last two paragraphs under the heading "You'll Eat Up the Prices of This Camp Cooking Gear!"

5. Move the last sentence at the end of the document to the end of the first full paragraph.

6. Reorder the items under the "RecTech Gear Up Ideas" heading by moving the first two product ideas to the end of the list.

7. Add bullets to the gear up product ideas.

8. Change the top margin to 2 inches.

9. Change the left margin to 1.75 inches.

10. Justify all the paragraphs in the document. (*Hint:* To select all paragraphs in the document at one time, click Edit on the menu bar, and then click Select All.)

11. Replace all occurrences of "RecTech" with "Rec-Tech."

12. Apply a 14-point sans serif font to each of the headings. Be sure to pick a font that looks professional and is easy to read.

13. Change the title's font to the same font you used for the headings, except set the size to 16 point.

14. Center and bold both lines of the title.

15. Bold the names and prices for all of the brand-name products in the Backpackers Guide.

16. Save, preview, and print the document, and then close the file.

4. Movie Review Your student newspaper has asked you to review four films currently showing in your area.

1. If neccessary, start Word, make sure your Student Disk is in the appropriate disk drive, and check your screen to make sure your settings match those in the tutorials.

2. Write a brief summary (1–2 paragraphs) for each movie and provide a rating for each movie. Correct any spelling errors. Save the document as Movie Review in the Tutorial 2 Cases folder on your Student Disk and print it.

Edit and format the document by doing the following:

3. Rearrange the order in which you discuss the movies to alphabetical order. (Remember to use the Undo and Redo buttons to correct any editing mistakes as you work.)

4. Change the top margin to 2 inches.

5. Set the left margin to 1.75 inches.

6. Add a title to your review, and then center and bold it.

7. Set the paragraph alignment to justify.

8. Italicize the title of each movie.

9. Save the edited document as Edited Movie Review.

10. Print the document.

11. Save and close your document.

Creating a Multiple-Page Report

Writing a Recommendation Report for AgriTechnology

OBJECTIVES

In this tutorial you will:

- Divide a document into sections
- Center a page between the top and bottom margins
- Create a header
- Number the pages in a document
- Attach a template and apply styles
- Create a table
- Add rows and shading to a table
- Widen table columns and align table text

CASE

AgriTechnology

Brittany Jones works for AgriTechnology, a biotechnology company that develops genetically engineered food products. Recently, AgriTechnology began shipping the EverRipe tomato to supermarkets. The EverRipe tomato is genetically engineered to stay ripe and fresh nearly twice as long as other varieties. Because of its longer shelf life and vine-ripened taste, supermarkets are eager to stock the new tomato, and the demand has been high. Unfortunately, the EverRipe tomato is also more susceptible to bruising than the usual varieties. Nearly 20 percent of the first year's crop was unmarketable because of damage sustained during shipping and handling. AgriTechnology's vice president, Ramon Espinoza, appointed Brittany to head a task force to determine how to increase the profitability of the EverRipe. The task force is ready to present the results of their study in the form of a report with an accompanying table. Brittany asks you to help prepare the report.

In this tutorial, you will format the report's title page so that it has a different layout from the rest of the report. The title page will contain only the title and subtitle, and will not have page numbers like the rest of the report. You will give the report a professional appearance quickly by applying a set of predefined formats that come with the Word program. You will also add a table to the AgriTechnology report that summarizes the task force's recommendations.

In this session you will review the task force's recommendation report. You will then learn how to divide a document into sections; center a page between the top and bottom margins; create a header; and number the pages in a document. Finally, you will learn how to attach a template and apply styles.

Planning the Document

As head of the task force, Brittany divided the responsibility for the report among the members of the group. Each person gathered information about one aspect of the problem and wrote the appropriate section of the report. Now Brittany must compile all the findings into a coherent and unified report. In addition, she must also follow the company's style guidelines for the content, organization, style, and format.

The report content includes the results of the study—obtained from interviews with other employees and visits to the packaging and distribution plant, trucking company, etc.—and recommendations for action.

Because Brittany knows some executives will not have time to read the entire report, she organized the report so it begins with an executive summary. The body of the report provides an in-depth statement of the problem and recommendations for solving that problem. At the end of the report, she summarizes the cost of the improvements.

The report's style follows established standards of business writing, emphasizing clarity, simplicity, and directness.

In accordance with AgriTechnology's style guide, Brittany's report will begin with a title page, with the text centered between the top and bottom margins. Every page except the title page will include a line of text at the top, giving a descriptive name for the report, as well as the page number. The text and headings will be formatted to look like all AgriTechnology's reports, following company guidelines for layout and text style.

At the end of the report, there will be a table that summarizes the costs of the proposed changes.

Opening the Draft of the Report

Brittany has already combined the individual sections into a draft of the report. You'll open the document and perform the formatting tasks indicated in Figure 3-1.

Figure 3-1 ◀
Initial draft of
task force's
report with
edits
(page 1)

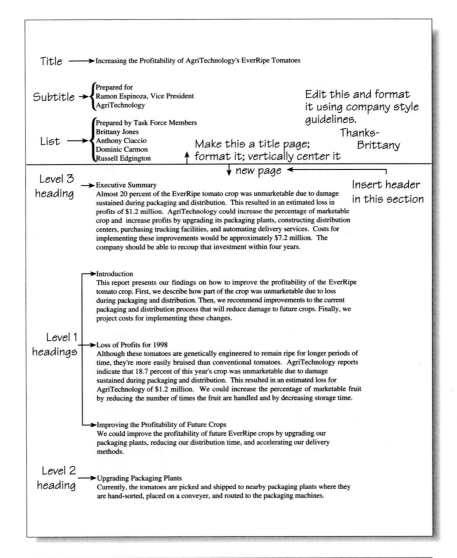

Figure 3-1 ◀
Initial draft of
task force's
report with
edits
(page 2)

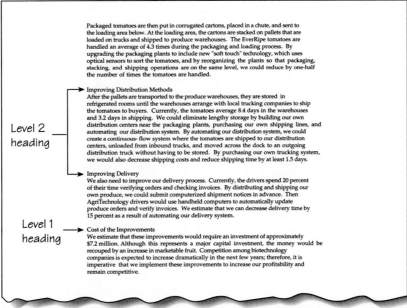

To open the document:

1. Start Word and place your Student Disk in the appropriate drive. Make sure your screen matches the figures in this tutorial. Because you'll be making large-scale formatting changes in this session, there is no need to display the nonprinting characters.

2. Open the file **EverRipe** from the **Tutorial.03** folder on your Student Disk.

3. To avoid altering the original file, save the document as **EverRipe Report** in the same folder.

Your first step is to change the layout of the title page.

Formatting the Document in Sections

According to the company guidelines, the title page of the report should be centered between the top and bottom margins of the page. In order to format the title page differently from the rest of the report, you need to divide the document into sections. A **section** is a unit or part of a document that can have its own page orientation, margins, headers, footers, and vertical alignment. Each section, in other words, is like a mini-document within a document.

To divide a document into sections, you insert a **section break**, a dotted line with the words "End of Section" that marks the point at which one section ends and another begins. Sections can start on a new page or continue on the same page. The easiest way to insert a section break is to use the Break command on the Insert menu.

To insert a section break after the title:

1. Position the insertion point immediately to the left of the "E" in the heading "Executive Summary." You want the text above this heading to be on a separate title page and the executive summary to begin the second page of the report.

2. Click **Insert** on the menu bar, and then click **Break** to open the Break dialog box. See Figure 3-2.

Figure 3-2 ◀
Break
dialog box

click here ————

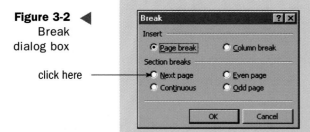

You can use this dialog box to insert several types of breaks into your document, including a page break, which places the text after it onto a new page. Instead of inserting a page break, however, you will insert a section break that indicates both a new section and a new page.

3. Click the **Next page** option button in the Section breaks area, and then click the **OK** button. A double-dotted line and the words "Section Break (Next Page)" appear before the heading "Executive Summary," indicating that you have inserted a section break. The status bar indicates that the insertion point is on page 2, section 2. See Figure 3-3.

Word

Figure 3-3 ◀
End of
section break

insertion point
in section 2

section number

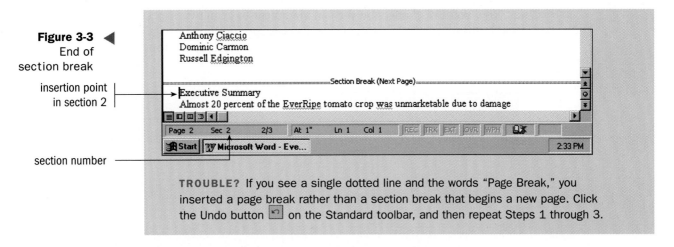

```
      Anthony Ciaccio
      Dominic Carmon
      Russell Edgington

─────────────────────Section Break (Next Page)─────────────────────
    ►Executive Summary
      Almost 20 percent of the EverRipe tomato crop was unmarketable due to damage

  Page 2    Sec 2    2/3    At 1"    Ln 1    Col 1    REC  TRK  EXT  OVR  WPH

  Start   W Microsoft Word - Eve...                              2:33 PM
```

TROUBLE? If you see a single dotted line and the words "Page Break," you inserted a page break rather than a section break that begins a new page. Click the Undo button ↰ on the Standard toolbar, and then repeat Steps 1 through 3.

Now that the title page is a separate section and page from the rest of the report, you can make changes affecting only that section, leaving the rest of the document intact.

Changing the Vertical Alignment of a Section

You're ready to center the title text vertically on the title page. But first you want to look at the layout of the report pages. To do this, you'll switch to the Print Preview window which shows the general layout of the report.

To see the document in Print Preview:

1. Click the **Print Preview** button ▣ on the Standard toolbar to open the Print Preview window.

2. If you only see one or two pages, click the **Multiple Pages** button ▦ on the Print Preview toolbar, and then click and drag across the top three pages in the drop-down box to select "1 × 3 Pages." The three pages of the report are reduced in size and appear side-by-side. See Figure 3-4. Although you cannot read the text on the pages, you can see their general layout.

Figure 3-4 ◀
Print Preview
of report

Print Preview toolbar

unformatted
title page

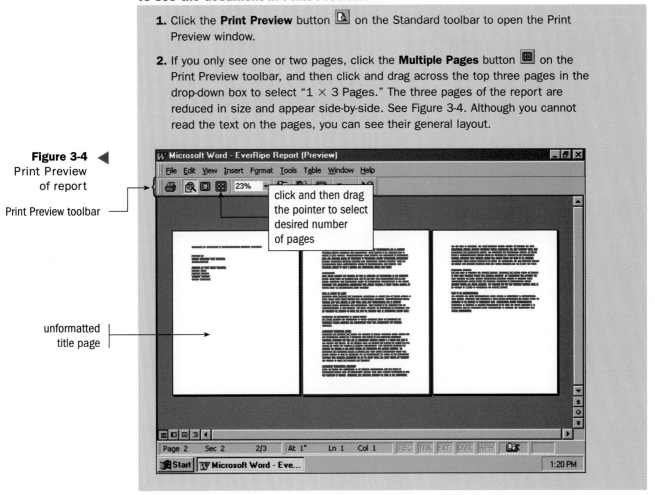

Now you can change the vertical alignment to center the lines of text between the top and bottom margins. The **vertical alignment** specifies how a page of text is positioned on the page between the top and bottom margins—flush at the top, flush at the bottom, or centered between the top and bottom margins.

REFERENCE window

VERTICALLY ALIGNING A SECTION

- Insert a section break to create a separate section for the page you want to align.
- Move the insertion point within the section you want to align.
- Click File on the menu bar, click Page Setup, click the Layout tab, and then select the alignment option you want.
- Make sure the Apply to list box displays the This section option.
- Click the OK button.

You'll center the title page text from within the Print Preview window.

To change the vertical alignment of the title page:

1. If the Magnifier button ⊕ is selected, click it once to deselect it.

2. Click the leftmost page in the Print Preview window to make sure the current page is page 1 (the title page). The status bar in the Print Preview window indicates the current page.

3. Click **File** on the menu bar, and then click **Page Setup** to open the Page Setup dialog box.

4. Click the **Layout** tab if it is not already selected. In the Apply to list box, click **This section** if it is not already selected so that the layout change affects only the first section, not both sections, of your document.

5. Click the **Vertical alignment** list arrow, and then click **Center** to center the pages of the current section—in this case just page 1—vertically between the top and bottom margins.

6. Click the **OK** button to return to the Print Preview window. The text of the title page is centered vertically, as shown in Figure 3-5.

Word

Figure 3-5 ◄
Title page
vertically
centered

text centered
between top and
bottom margins

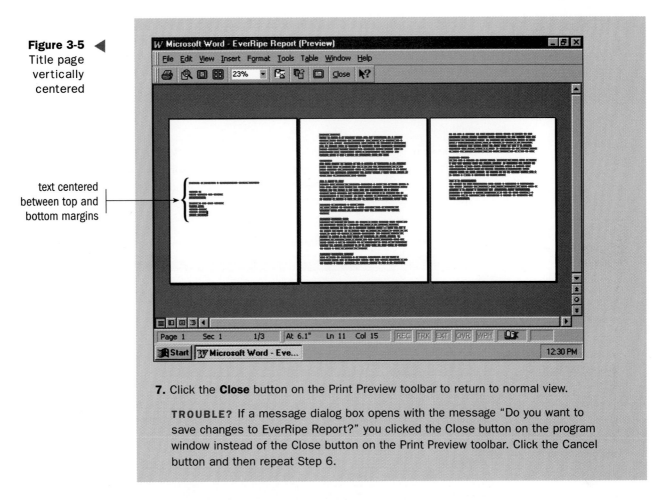

7. Click the **Close** button on the Print Preview toolbar to return to normal view.

TROUBLE? If a message dialog box opens with the message "Do you want to save changes to EverRipe Report?" you clicked the Close button on the program window instead of the Close button on the Print Preview toolbar. Click the Cancel button and then repeat Step 6.

You have successfully centered the title page text. Next, you turn your attention to placing a descriptive name for the report and the page number at the top of every page.

Adding Headers

The AgriTechnology report guidelines require a short report title and the page number to be printed at the top of every page except the title page. Text that is printed at the top of every page is called a **header**. For example, the section name, tutorial number, and page number printed at the top of the page you are reading is a header. Similarly, a **footer** is text that is printed at the bottom of every page. (You'll have a chance to work with footers in the Tutorial Assignments at the end of this tutorial.)

When you insert a header or footer into a document, you switch to Header and Footer view. The Header and Footer toolbar is displayed and the insertion point moves to the top of the document, where the header will appear. The main text is dimmed, indicating that it cannot be edited until you return to normal or page layout view.

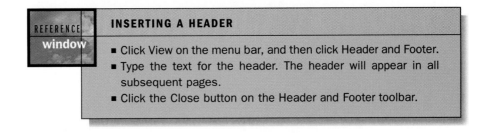

REFERENCE
window

INSERTING A HEADER

■ Click View on the menu bar, and then click Header and Footer.
■ Type the text for the header. The header will appear in all subsequent pages.
■ Click the Close button on the Header and Footer toolbar.

You'll create a header for the main body of the report (section 2) that prints "EverRipe Recommendation Report" at the left margin and the page number at the right margin.

To insert a header for section 2:

1. Make sure the insertion point is anywhere after the heading "Executive Summary" on page 2 so that the insertion point is in section 2 and not in section 1.

2. Click **View** on the menu bar, and then click **Header and Footer**. The screen changes to Header and Footer view, and the Header and Footer toolbar appears in the document window. The header area appears in the top margin of your document surrounded by a dashed line and displays the words "Header -Section 2-." See Figure 3-6.

Figure 3-6 ◀
Creating
a header

header area ——

Header and
Footer toolbar ——

Same as Previous
button pressed ——

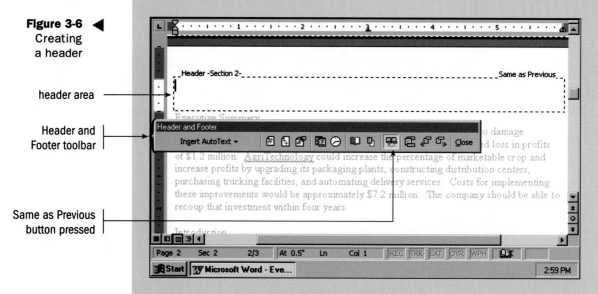

TROUBLE? If the header area displays "Header -Section 1-," click the Show Next button 🔲 on the Header and Footer toolbar until the header area displays "Header -Section 2-."

TROUBLE? If the main text of the document doesn't appear on the screen, click the Show/Hide Document Text button 🔲 on the Header and Footer toolbar, and continue with Step 3.

TROUBLE? If the Header and Footer toolbar covers the header area, drag the toolbar below the header area, similar to the position shown in Figure 3-6.

3. Click the **Same as Previous** button 🔲 on the Header and Footer toolbar so that the button is not pressed. This ensures that the text of the current header will apply only to the current section (section 2), not to the previous section (section 1) also.

4. Type **EverRipe Recommendation Report**. The title is automatically aligned on the left. See Figure 3-7.

Figure 3-7 ◀
Text of header

report title ——→

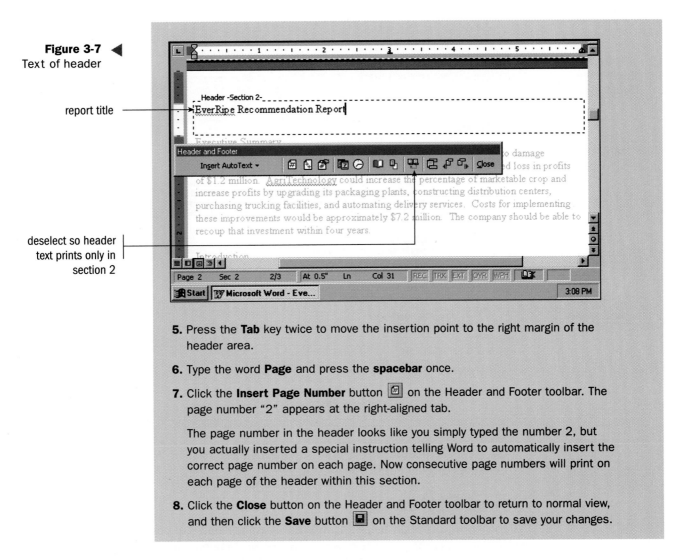

deselect so header
text prints only in
section 2

5. Press the **Tab** key twice to move the insertion point to the right margin of the header area.

6. Type the word **Page** and press the **spacebar** once.

7. Click the **Insert Page Number** button ⊞ on the Header and Footer toolbar. The page number "2" appears at the right-aligned tab.

The page number in the header looks like you simply typed the number 2, but you actually inserted a special instruction telling Word to automatically insert the correct page number on each page. Now consecutive page numbers will print on each page of the header within this section.

8. Click the **Close** button on the Header and Footer toolbar to return to normal view, and then click the **Save** button ⊞ on the Standard toolbar to save your changes.

Notice that you can't see the header in normal view. To see exactly how the header will appear on the printed page, you can switch to page layout view, which lets you read the headers and footers as well as see the margins.

To view the header and margins in page layout view:

1. Click the **Page Layout View** button ▣.

2. Click the **Zoom Control** list arrow on the Standard toolbar, and then click **75%**. You can now see the header and the page margins. Next, you'll use the browse buttons to examine each page.

3. Click the **Select Browse Object** button ▣ below the vertical scroll bar and click the Browse by Page button ▢. The cursor moves to the top of the third page.

4. Click the **Previous Page** button ≛ (just below the vertical scroll bar) twice to move to page 1.

5. Click the **Next Page** button ≛ to move to the top of the second page.

6. Click the **Next Page** button ≛ again to move to the top of the third page. Notice that the header appears on pages 2 and 3 but not the title page. See Figure 3-8.

Figure 3-8 ◄
Header in page
layout view

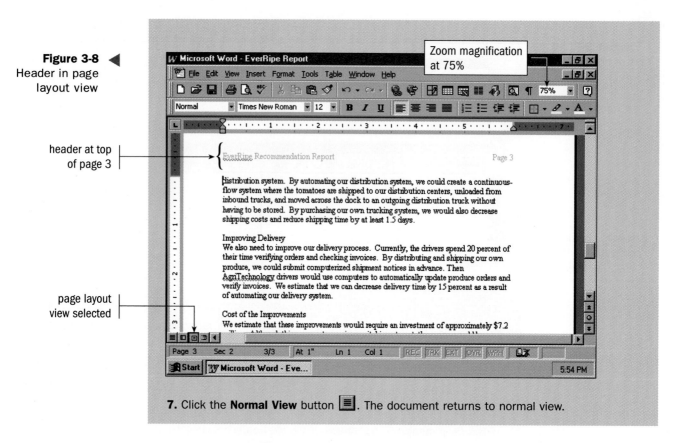

header at top
of page 3

page layout
view selected

7. Click the **Normal View** button 🔲. The document returns to normal view.

The recommendation report now has the required header. Your next job is to make style changes throughout the document.

Using Styles

As you know, it's often helpful to use the Format Painter to copy formatting from one paragraph to another. However, when you are working on a longer document, you'll find it easier to use a set of formats known as a **style**. Every Word document opens with a set of predefined styles which include: Normal (the default style for paragraphs in a Word document), Heading 1, Heading 2, and Heading 3. Word's default Normal style is defined as 10 point Times New Roman, left alignment, with single-line spacing. You can modify any of the predefined styles to suit the needs of your document, as you did when you changed the font size to 12 point at the beginning of the first tutorial.

The style of the current paragraph (the paragraph where the cursor is located) appears in the Style list box on the Formatting toolbar. All available styles are listed in the Style list, as shown in Figure 3-9. Styles affecting individual characters appear with a letter "a" in the gray box to the right of the style name (for example, the Page Number style in Figure 3-9); paragraph styles appear with the paragraph icon in the gray box (for example, the Heading 1 style in Figure 3-9). The font size of each style is also displayed. For example, the Page Number style is 10 point. All styles in the list appear with the formatting characteristics applied so you can see what they look like before choosing one.

Figure 3-9 ◄
List of available
default styles

click to display
list of styles

current style

font size

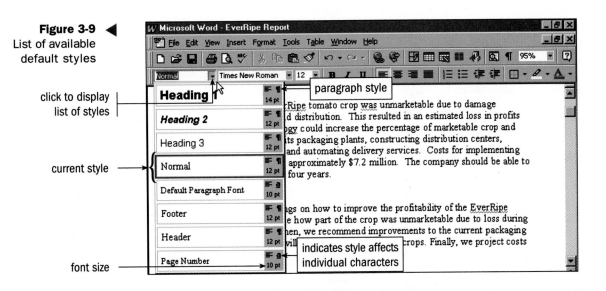

Attaching a Template to a Document

You can change the available styles by using a different template. A **template** is a set of predefined styles designed for a specific type of document. For example, Word provides templates for formatting reports, brochures, memos, letters, or resumes, among others. Word's default template, the Normal template, contains the Normal paragraph style described earlier.

There are two steps to using a template. First you need to attach the template to the document. Then you need to apply the template's styles to the various parts of the document. You'll begin by attaching a new template to the EverRipe Report document.

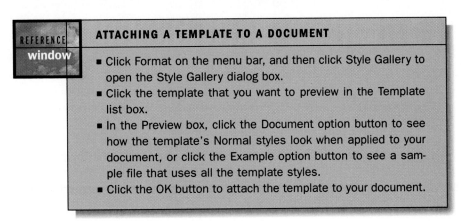

REFERENCE
window

ATTACHING A TEMPLATE TO A DOCUMENT

- Click Format on the menu bar, and then click Style Gallery to open the Style Gallery dialog box.
- Click the template that you want to preview in the Template list box.
- In the Preview box, click the Document option button to see how the template's Normal styles look when applied to your document, or click the Example option button to see a sample file that uses all the template styles.
- Click the OK button to attach the template to your document.

Brittany tells you that all reports produced at the company use Word's predefined Professional Report template. She suggests you preview the template to see what it looks like, and then attach it to the recommendation report. You'll use the Style Gallery to do this.

To preview and attach the Professional Report template to your document:

1. Click **Format** on the menu bar, and then click **Style Gallery** to open the Style Gallery dialog box. The recommendation report appears in the Preview of window and "(current)" appears in the Template list box. The report appears formatted the same way as it is in the document window.

2. Scroll to and then click **Professional Report** in the Template list box to select the template. In the Preview of Report window, the text of your document changes to reflect the new Normal style for the Professional Report template. See Figure 3-10.

Figure 3-10 ◀
Style Gallery
with preview of
Professional
Report
template

selected template ⟶

click to see
sample document

preview of document ⟶

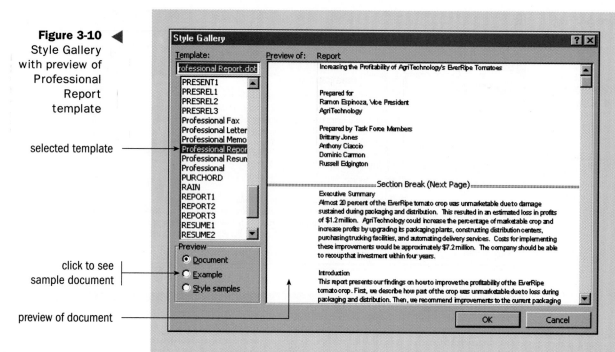

3. In the Preview box, click the **Example** option button to see a sample document that uses all the Professional Report template styles. Scroll through the sample document to preview all the styles that are available to you in this template.

4. Click the **OK** button to attach the template to the report and return to the document window. The template's default font (10-point Arial) and paragraph indentation are applied to the entire document, because the text in the document has been formatted with the Normal style, and because no other styles, such as a Heading style, have been applied to the text at this point. You'll see the Professional Report template styles when you apply them in the next section.

5. Click the **Style** list arrow on the Formatting toolbar. Scroll through the style list to verify that the styles of the Professional Report template are now available in this document, and then click the **Style** list arrow again to close the style list.

At this point, the only apparent change in the text is that the font changed from 12 point Times New Roman to 10 point Arial and that the paragraphs are left-indented 0.75 inch. (On some computers, the 10 point Arial is also condensed so that the font is actually Arial Narrow.) Now that the Professional Report template is attached to the report, you can begin applying its styles to the document.

Applying Styles

The best way to apply a template's styles to a document is to highlight individual parts of the document, and then select the appropriate style from the Style list on the Formatting toolbar. For example, to format the report title, you would highlight "Increasing the Profitability of AgriTechnology's EverRipe Tomatoes" on the title page, and then select the Title Cover style from the Style list.

You'll apply the Professional Report template styles now, beginning with the report title.

To apply styles to the report document:

1. Scroll to the title page, and then drag the pointer to select the title **Increasing the Profitability of AgriTechnology's EverRipe Tomatoes**.

2. Click the **Style** list arrow on the Formatting toolbar to open the Style list. Scroll down the list, and then click **Title Cover**. Word applies the style to the selected text. Notice that the font of the Title Cover style is 32 point Arial Black.

3. Deselect the text. See Figure 3-11. Notice that the Title Cover style dramatically emphasizes the title. You'll get a better idea of its positioning on the page when you preview and print the document.

Figure 3-11 ◀
Title formatted
with Title
Cover style

formatted text ⟶

unformatted text ⟶

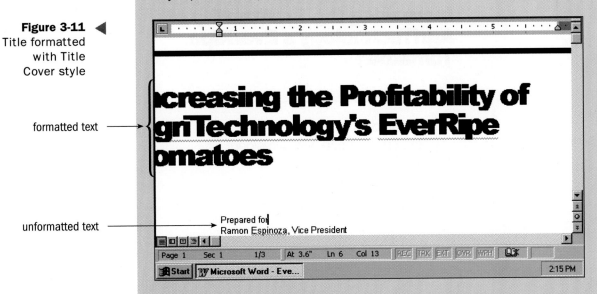

4. Continue formatting the rest of the document by selecting text and applying the styles indicated in Figure 3-12. Keep in mind that you do not have to apply a new style to any text not labeled in Figure 3-12, because Word already applied the Normal style for the Professional template when you attached it to the document. Be careful to choose List 2 when formatting the name list; there are several list and list continuation styles in this template, each with a different indent. Use the Undo button to undo any mistakes. To repeat applying a style you just applied, press the F4 key. When you are finished, your document should look similar to Figure 3-12. You might not be able to see the gray background of the Block Quotation style until you print the document.

Figure 3-12 ◀
Formatted
version of
recommenda-
tion report
(title page)

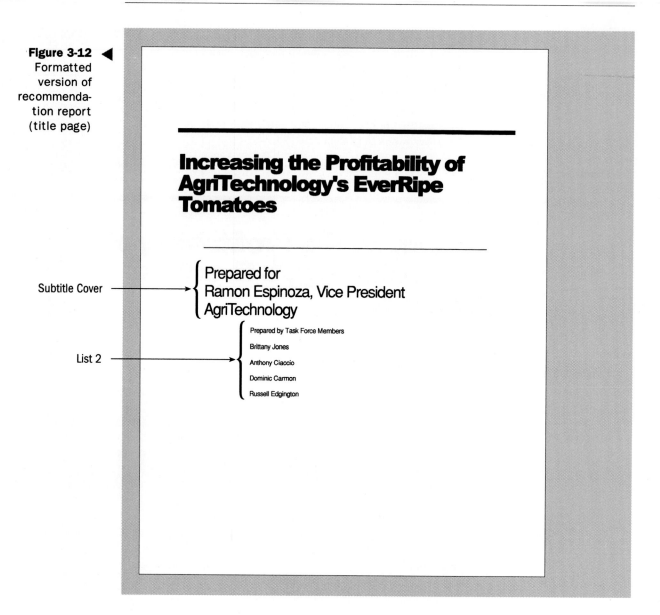

Increasing the Profitability of AgriTechnology's EverRipe Tomatoes

Subtitle Cover ────▶ Prepared for
Ramon Espinoza, Vice President
AgriTechnology

List 2 ────▶ Prepared by Task Force Members
Brittany Jones
Anthony Ciaccio
Dominic Carmon
Russell Edgington

Word

Figure 3-12 ◀
Formatted
version of
recommenda-
tion report
(page 2)

Heading 3

Block Quotation

Heading 1

Heading 1

Heading 1

Heading 2

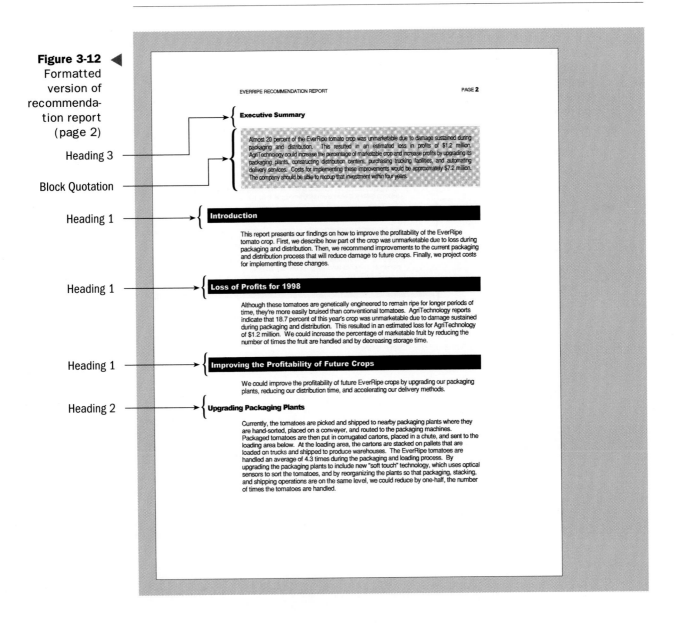

Figure 3-12 ◀
Formatted
version of
recommenda-
tion report
(page 3)

Heading 2 ——

Heading 2 ——

Heading 1 ——

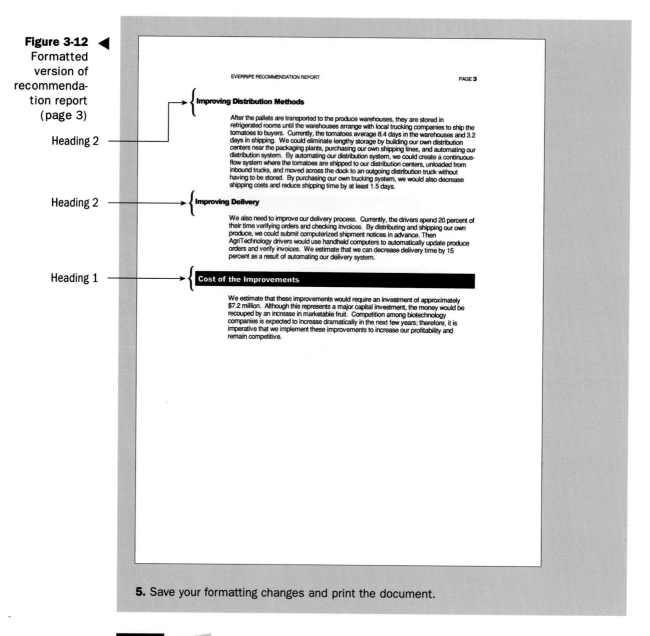

EVERRIPE RECOMMENDATION REPORT   PAGE **3**

Improving Distribution Methods

After the pallets are transported to the produce warehouses, they are stored in refrigerated rooms until the warehouses arrange with local trucking companies to ship the tomatoes to buyers. Currently, the tomatoes average 8.4 days in the warehouses and 3.2 days in shipping. We could eliminate lengthy storage by building our own distribution centers near the packaging plants, purchasing our own shipping lines, and automating our distribution system. By automating our distribution system, we could create a continuous-flow system where the tomatoes are shipped to our distribution centers, unloaded from inbound trucks, and moved across the dock to an outgoing distribution truck without having to be stored. By purchasing our own trucking system, we would also decrease shipping costs and reduce shipping time by at least 1.5 days.

Improving Delivery

We also need to improve our delivery process. Currently, the drivers spend 20 percent of their time verifying orders and checking invoices. By distributing and shipping our own produce, we could submit computerized shipment notices in advance. Then AgriTechnology drivers would use handheld computers to automatically update produce orders and verify invoices. We estimate that we can decrease delivery time by 15 percent as a result of automating our delivery system.

Cost of the Improvements

We estimate that these improvements would require an investment of approximately $7.2 million. Although this represents a major capital investment, the money would be recouped by an increase in marketable fruit. Competition among biotechnology companies is expected to increase dramatically in the next few years; therefore, it is imperative that we implement these improvements to increase our profitability and remain competitive.

5. Save your formatting changes and print the document.

Quick Check

1 Define the following in your own words:
   a. style
   b. template
   c. Style list
   d. section (of a document)
   e. vertical alignment
   f. header

2 Why would you need to insert a section break into a document?

3 Explain how to center the title page vertically between the top and bottom margins.

4 What is the difference between a header and a footer?

5 How do you insert the page number in a header?

6 What are the two steps involved in using a new template?

7. How do you attach a template to a document?

8. Explain how you applied styles to the EverRipe Report document.

You have planned, formatted, and printed Brittany's recommendation report so that the results are professional-looking, clearly presented, and easy to read. You have done this using the Word features that quickly add formatting to an entire section of a document: headers, templates, and styles. Next you will add and format a table that summarizes the costs and benefits of the task force's recommendations.

SESSION

3.2

In this session you will learn how to add a table to the report. Then you'll add rows to the table, widen the columns in the table, and align the text in the table. Finally you'll add shading to make the table look more professional.

Inserting Tables

The Word Table feature allows you to quickly organize data and to arrange text in an easy-to-read format of columns and rows. Figure 3-13 summarizes the elements of a Word table.

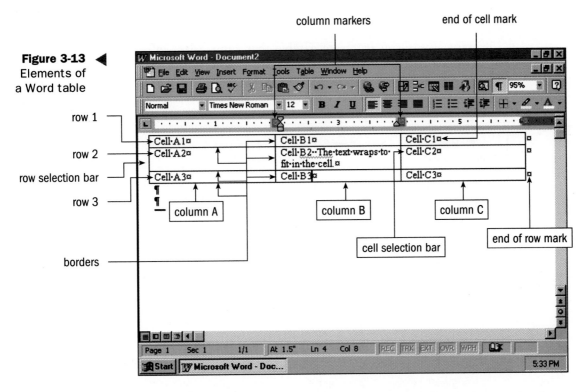

Figure 3-13
Elements of
a Word table

A **table** is information arranged in horizontal rows and vertical columns. As you can see by looking through this book, a table is an efficient way of communicating a lot of information in an easy-to-read format. It's convenient to refer to table rows as if they were labeled with numbers (row 1 at the top, row 2 below row 1, and so forth), and each column as a letter (column A on the far left, column B to the right of column A, and so forth). However, you do not see row and column numbers on the screen.

The area where a row and column intersect is called a **cell**. Each cell is identified by a column and row label. For example, the cell in the upper-left corner of a table is cell A1 (column A, row 1), the cell to the right of that is cell B1, the cell below cell A1 is A2, and so forth. The table's structure is indicated by **borders**, which are lines that outline the rows and columns. With Word's Table feature, you can create a blank table and then insert information into it, or you can convert existing text into a table. You'll begin with a blank table in the next section. In the Tutorial Assignments at the end of this tutorial, you'll have a chance to convert text into a table.

Creating a Table Using the Insert Table Button

The easiest way to create a table is by moving the insertion point to the location in your document where you want a table, clicking the Insert Table button on the Standard toolbar, and then specifying the number of rows and columns you need in your table. Word inserts a blank table structure with the number of rows and columns you specified.

REFERENCE window

CREATING A BLANK TABLE USING THE INSERT TABLE BUTTON

- Place the insertion point where you want the table to appear in the document.
- Click the Insert Table button on the Standard toolbar to display a drop-down grid.
- Drag the pointer to select the desired number of rows and columns, and then release the mouse button.

Brittany wants you to create a table that summarizes information in the EverRipe report, which you formatted in the previous session. Figure 3-14 shows a sketch of what Brittany wants the table to look like. The table will allow AgriTechnology's executives to see at a glance the cost and benefits of each improvement.

Figure 3-14 ◀
Sketch of
EverRipe table

Projected Improvement	Initial Cost	Percent of Total Cost	Benefit
Upgrade packaging plants	$2,500,000	35%	Reduce by one-half the number of times tomatoes are handled
Improve distribution methods	$3,700,000	51%	Decrease shipping costs and reduce shipping time by 1.5 days
Automate delivery paperwork	$1,000,000	14%	Decrease delivery time by 15%
Total	$7,200,000		

You'll use the Insert Table button to create the table.

To create a blank table using the Insert Table button:

1. If you took a break after the last session, make sure Word is running and that the EverRipe Report document is open. Because you will be working with table formatting elements in this session, make sure the nonprinting characters are displayed.

2. Position the insertion point at the end of the last paragraph in the report, and press the **Enter** key twice to insert a space between the text and the table. Word inserts the table at the location of the insertion point.

3. Click the **Insert Table** button on the Standard toolbar. A drop-down grid resembling a miniature table appears below the Insert Table button. The grid initially has four rows and five columns. You can drag the pointer to extend the grid to as many rows and columns as you need. In this case, you need only four rows and four columns.

4. Position the pointer in the upper-left cell of the grid, and then click and drag the pointer down and across the grid until you highlight four rows and four columns. As you drag the pointer across the grid, Word indicates the size of the table (rows by columns) at the bottom of the grid. See Figure 3-15.

click to insert table

Figure 3-15 ◄
Insert
Table grid

drag to select
table size

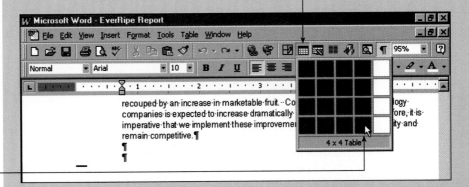

5. Release the mouse button. An empty table, four rows by four columns, appears in your document with the insertion point blinking in the upper-left corner (cell A1).

The table is outlined with borders, and the four columns are of equal width. The column widths are indicated by **column markers** on the ruler. Each cell contains an end-of-cell mark, and each row contains an end-of-row mark.

TROUBLE? If you don't see the end-of-cell and end-of-row marks, you need to show nonprinting characters. Click the Show/Hide ¶ button ¶ on the Standard toolbar to show nonprinting characters.

Now that you've created the table, you are ready to enter text and numbers summarizing the EverRipe report.

Entering Text in a Table

You can enter text in a table by moving the insertion point to a cell and typing. If the text takes up more than one line in the cell, Word automatically wraps the text to the next line and increases the height of that cell and all the cells in that row. To move the insertion point to the next cell to the right, you can either click in that cell or press the Tab key. If you want to return to the previous cell, you can press and hold down the Shift key while you press the Tab key. Figure 3-16 summarizes the keystrokes for moving within a table.

Figure 3-16 ◄
Keystrokes for
moving around
a table

Press	To move the insertion point
Tab or →	One cell to the right, or to the first cell in the next row
Shift + Tab or ←	One cell to the left, or to the last cell in the previous row
Alt + Home	To first cell of current row
Alt + End	To last cell of current row
Alt + PageUp	To top cell or current column
Alt + PageDown	To bottom cell of current column
↑	One cell up in current column
↓	One cell down in current column

Now you are ready to insert information into the table.

To insert data into the table:

1. Make sure the insertion point is in cell A1 of the table.

2. Type **Projected Improvement**. Watch the end-of-cell mark move to the right as you type.

3. Press the **Tab** key to move to cell B1. See Figure 3-17.

Figure 3-17 ◄
Adding text
to the table

end-of-cell mark ——

new text ——

insertion point
in cell B1

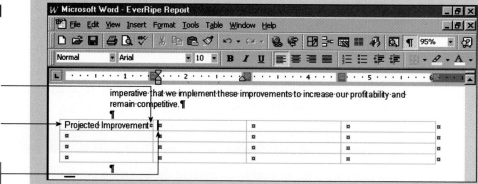

TROUBLE? If you accidentally pressed the Enter key instead of the Tab key, Word created a new paragraph within cell A1 rather than moving the insertion point to cell B1. Press the Backspace key to remove the paragraph mark, and then press the Tab key to move to cell B1.

4. Type **Initial Cost** and then press the **Tab** key to move to cell C1.

5. Type **Percent of Total Cost** and then press the **Tab** key to move to cell D1.

6. Type **Benefit** and then press the **Tab** key to move the insertion point from cell D1 to cell A2. Notice that when you press the Tab key in the last column of the table, the insertion point moves to the first column in the next row.

You have entered the **heading row**, the row that identifies the information in each column.

7. Type the remaining information for the table, as shown in Figure 3-18, pressing the Tab key to move from cell to cell.

Figure 3-18
Table with
completed
information

heading row

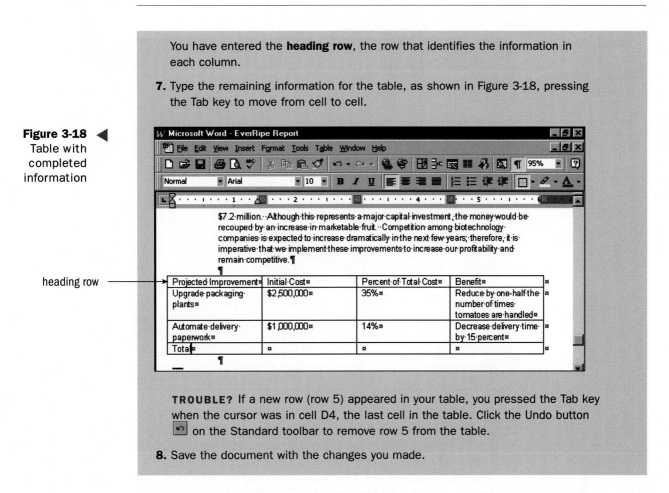

TROUBLE? If a new row (row 5) appeared in your table, you pressed the Tab key when the cursor was in cell D4, the last cell in the table. Click the Undo button on the Standard toolbar to remove row 5 from the table.

8. Save the document with the changes you made.

Keep in mind that many of the methods you've used to edit a document, such as the Backspace key, the copy-and-paste feature, the Undo button, and the AutoCorrect feature, work the same way in a table. Just like in a paragraph, you must select text within a table in order to edit it.

Inserting Additional Rows

When creating a table, you might be unsure about how many rows or columns you will actually need. You might need to delete extra rows and columns, or, as in this case, you might need to add them. Either way, you can easily modify an existing table's structure. Figure 3-19 summarizes ways to insert or delete rows and columns in a table.

Figure 3-19 ◀
Ways to insert
or delete table
rows and
columns

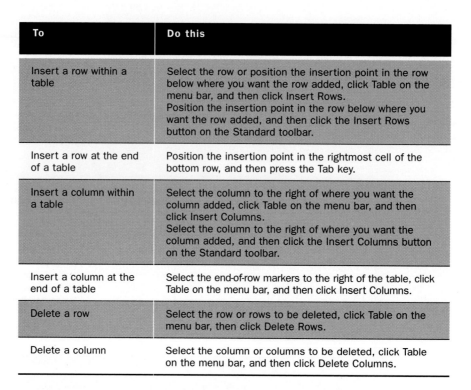

To	Do this
Insert a row within a table	Select the row or position the insertion point in the row below where you want the row added, click Table on the menu bar, and then click Insert Rows. Position the insertion point in the row below where you want the row added, and then click the Insert Rows button on the Standard toolbar.
Insert a row at the end of a table	Position the insertion point in the rightmost cell of the bottom row, and then press the Tab key.
Insert a column within a table	Select the column to the right of where you want the column added, click Table on the menu bar, and then click Insert Columns. Select the column to the right of where you want the column added, and then click the Insert Columns button on the Standard toolbar.
Insert a column at the end of a table	Select the end-of-row markers to the right of the table, click Table on the menu bar, and then click Insert Columns.
Delete a row	Select the row or rows to be deleted, click Table on the menu bar, then click Delete Rows.
Delete a column	Select the column or columns to be deleted, click Table on the menu bar, and then click Delete Columns.

Word allows you to insert additional rows either within or at the end of a table. You can insert a row or rows within the table with the Insert Rows command on the Table menu. To insert a row at the end of the table, you simply place the insertion point in the last cell of the last row and press the Tab key.

After looking over the EverRipe table, you see that you forgot to include a row on improving distribution methods. You'll insert that row and the relevant data now using the Insert Rows command, which inserts a row above the current row. To insert a row above the "Automate delivery paperwork" row (row 3), you begin by selecting that row. You will insert the new row using the Table shortcut menu, which contains frequently used table commands.

To insert a row within the table:

1. Position the pointer in the margin next to cell A3 (which contains the text "Automate delivery paperwork"). This area is called the row **selection bar**. The pointer changes to ⟋ .

2. Click to select row 3.

3. With the pointer ⟩ positioned anywhere over the selected row, click the right mouse button. The Table shortcut menu opens. Notice that the shortcut menu includes a Delete Rows command, which you could use if you needed to delete the selected row. In this case, however, you want to insert a row. See Figure 3-20.

Figure 3-20 ◀
Table shortcut
menu

click to insert
a new row

click to delete the
selected row

click here to
select row

right-click over
highlighted
row to display
shortcut menu

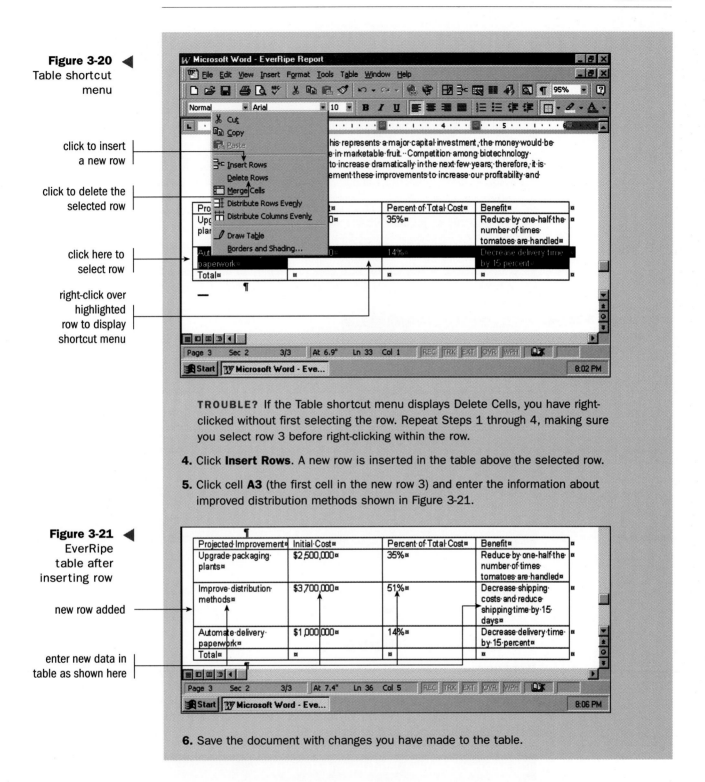

TROUBLE? If the Table shortcut menu displays Delete Cells, you have right-clicked without first selecting the row. Repeat Steps 1 through 4, making sure you select row 3 before right-clicking within the row.

4. Click **Insert Rows**. A new row is inserted in the table above the selected row.

5. Click cell **A3** (the first cell in the new row 3) and enter the information about improved distribution methods shown in Figure 3-21.

Figure 3-21 ◀
EverRipe
table after
inserting row

new row added

enter new data in
table as shown here

Projected Improvement	Initial Cost	Percent of Total Cost	Benefit	
Upgrade packaging plants	$2,500,000	35%	Reduce by one-half the number of times tomatoes are handled	
Improve distribution methods	$3,700,000	51%	Decrease shipping costs and reduce shipping time by 15 days	
Automate delivery paperwork	$1,000,000	14%	Decrease delivery time by 15 percent	
Total				

6. Save the document with changes you have made to the table.

Using AutoSum to Total a Table Column

Rather than calculating column totals by hand and entering them, you can easily have Word compute the totals of numeric columns in a table.

To total the values in the Cost column:

1. Click cell **B5**, the last call in the Initial Cost column.

2. Click the **Tables and Borders** button ⊞ on the Standard toolbar. The Tables and Borders toolbar appears and the document automatically changes to page layout view.

   TROUBLE? If the Office Assistant opens, displaying a hint on working with this window, just click the Cancel button to close the Office Assistant.

3. Click the **AutoSum** button Σ on the Tables and Borders toolbar. The total of the column appears in cell B5 formatted with a dollar sign and two decimal places. You want it to match the numbers above it, so you'll delete the decimal point and the two zeroes.

4. Click **Table** on the menu bar, and then click **Formula**.

5. Click the **Number Format** list arrow, and select the only format with a dollar sign.

6. In the Number Format text box, click to the right of the format and press the **Backspace** key until only $#, ##0 remains, as shown in Figure 3-22.

Figure 3-22 ◀
Formula dialog
box after
adjusting
number format

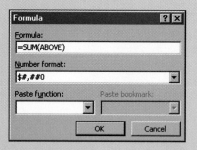

7. Click **OK**. The Initial Cost total is now formatted like the numbers above it.

8. Click the **Close** button ✗ on the Tables and Borders toolbar. If it is docked below the Formatting toolbar, and does not have a Close button, right click the toolbar and click Tables and Borders to remove the checkmark next to it.

9. Click the **Normal View** button ▤.

You have finished creating the tables and entering data. Now you can concentrate on improving the table's appearance.

Formatting Tables

Word provides a variety of ways to enhance the appearance of the tables you create: you can alter the width of the columns and the height of the rows, or change the alignment of text within the cells or the alignment of the table between the left and right margins.

After reviewing your work, Brittany decides the EverRipe table needs formatting to make it more attractive and easier to read.

Changing Column Width and Height

Sometimes you'll want to adjust the column widths in a table in order to make the text easier to read. If you want to specify an exact width for a column, you should use the Cell Height and Width command on the Table menu. However, it's usually easiest simply to drag the column's right-hand border to a new position.

Word

The Initial Cost column (column B) and the Percent of Total Cost column (column C) are too wide for the information they contain and should be decreased. Also, the Benefit column (column D) would be easier to read if it was a little wider. You'll change these widths by dragging the column borders, using the ruler as a guide. Keep in mind that to change the width of a column, you need to drag the column's rightmost border.

To change the width of columns by dragging the borders:

1. Position the insertion point anywhere in the EverRipe table. Make sure you do not select any cells.

2. Move the pointer over the border between columns B and C (in other words, over the rightmost border of column B). The pointer changes to ✛ .

3. Click and drag the pointer to the left until the border reaches 2.5 inches on the ruler, and then release the mouse button. Notice that as the second column decreases in width, the width of column C increases, but the overall width of the table does not change. See Figure 3-23.

Figure 3-23 ◀
Table after decreasing the width of column B

drag this pointer to change the column width

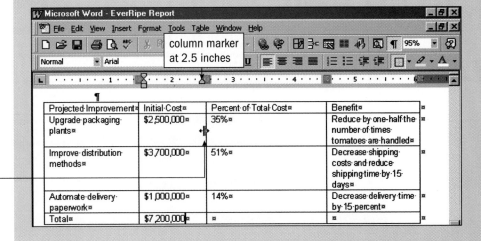

4. Click and drag the right border of column C to the left until it reaches about 3.5 inches on the ruler. Notice that Word automatically adjusted column D to compensate for the changes in columns B and C. Instead of being crowded onto several short lines, the text in column D is stretched out into one or two longer, easier-to-read lines. This means you don't have to worry about widening the last column.

You can change the height of rows by dragging a row border, just as you changed column widths by dragging a column border. You'll make row 1 taller to make it more prominent. To do this you have to change to page layout view.

To change the height of row 1:

1. Click the **Page Layout View** button 🔳.

2. Position the pointer over the bottom border of the heading row. The pointer changes to ⬍.

3. Drag the row border downward about ¼".

4. Click the **Normal View** button 🔳.

The EverRipe table now looks much better with its new column widths and row height. Next you'll align the text to make the table even more attractive.

Aligning Text Within Cells

Aligning the text within the cells of a table makes the information easier to read. For example, aligning numbers and percentages along the right margin helps the reader to quickly compare the values. Centering the headings makes the columns more visually appealing. You can align text within the cells the same way you do other text—with the alignment buttons on the Formatting toolbar.

The dollar and percentage amounts in columns B and C would be much easier to read if you were to align the numbers on the right side of the cells. The table would also look better with the headings centered.

To right-align the numerical data and center the headings:

1. Drag the pointer to select cells **B2** through **C5**. See Figure 3-24.

Figure 3-24 ◀
Selected data

selected cells are currently left-aligned

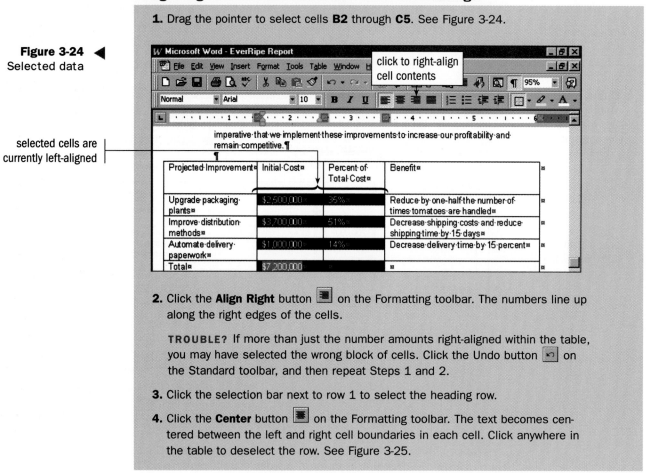

2. Click the **Align Right** button 📄 on the Formatting toolbar. The numbers line up along the right edges of the cells.

   TROUBLE? If more than just the number amounts right-aligned within the table, you may have selected the wrong block of cells. Click the Undo button 🔙 on the Standard toolbar, and then repeat Steps 1 and 2.

3. Click the selection bar next to row 1 to select the heading row.

4. Click the **Center** button 📄 on the Formatting toolbar. The text becomes centered between the left and right cell boundaries in each cell. Click anywhere in the table to deselect the row. See Figure 3-25.

Word

Figure 3-25 ◄
Table
with newly
aligned text

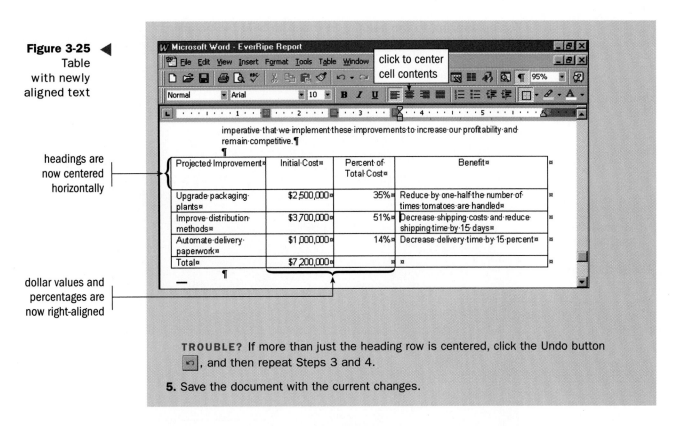

headings are
now centered
horizontally

dollar values and
percentages are
now right-aligned

TROUBLE? If more than just the heading row is centered, click the Undo button ↶, and then repeat Steps 3 and 4.

5. Save the document with the current changes.

The tables look better with the headings centered and the numbers right-aligned. Now you'll vertically align the text in the heading row so that it is centered between the top and bottom lines.

To align the text in the heading row vertically:

1. Click to the left of row 1 to select the heading row of the table.

2. Click the **Tables and Borders** button ▦ on the Standard toolbar.

3. Click the **Center Vertically** button ▤ on the Tables and Borders toolbar. The text becomes vertically centered in the row.

4. Close the Tables and Borders toolbar, and then click anywhere in the document to deselect the row.

5. Click the **Normal View** button ▤.

You'll finish formatting the table by adding shading to the cells containing the headings.

Adding Shading

With the Borders and Shading dialog box, adding **shading** (a gray or colored background) to any text in a document is a simple task. Shading is especially useful in tables when you want to emphasize headings, totals, or other important items. In most cases, when you add shading to a table, you'll also need to bold the shaded text to make it easier to read.

You'll add a light gray shading to the heading row. You'll also bold the headings. As with most formatting tasks, you'll begin by selecting the row you want to format, and then you'll open the Borders and Shading dialog box, which is a good way to make several formatting changes at once.

To add shading to the heading row and to bold the headings:

1. Click to the left of row 1 to select the heading row of the table.

2. Click **Format** on the menu bar, and then click **Borders and Shading**. The Borders and Shading dialog box opens.

3. Click the **Shading** tab to display a list of shading options. The Fill section displays the available colors and shades of gray that you can use to shade the heading row.

4. Click the **top right square**. The label Gray-12.5% appears to the right of the color selections, and the Preview section on the right shows a sample. See Figure 3-26.

Figure 3-26 ◄
Shading tab

click this 12.5% gray ────

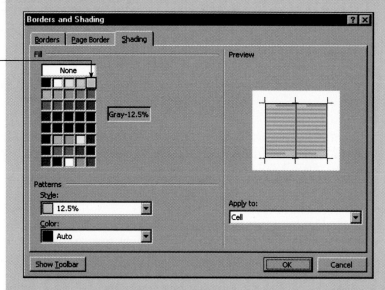

5. Click the **OK** button. A light gray background appears in the heading row. Now you need to bold the text to make the headings stand out from the shading.

6. Click the **Bold** button **B** on the Formatting toolbar to bold the headings.

   TROUBLE? If any of the headings break incorrectly (for example, if the "t" in "Cost" moves to its own line), you might need to widen columns to accommodate the bolded letters. Drag the column borders as necessary to adjust the column widths so that all the column headings are displayed correctly.

7. Click in the selection bar next to the last row to select the Total row.

8. Click the **Bold** button on the formatting toolbar to bold the total.

9. Click anywhere outside the total row to deselect it and then save your changes. Your completed table should look like Figure 3-27.

Figure 3-27
Bolded
headings
with shading

newly formatted
heading row

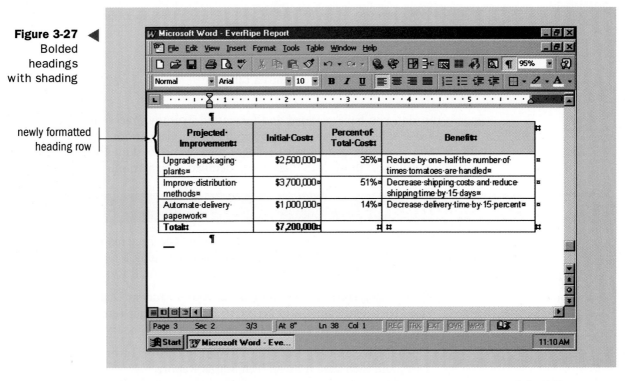

Now that you're finished with the EverRipe table, you print a copy of the full report to give to Brittany. You'll preview the report first to make sure the table fits on the third page.

To preview the table:

1. Click the **Print Preview** button on the Standard toolbar to open the Print Preview window.

2. Make sure the Magnifier button is selected and then click the table. The table looks fine, so you decide to print the report.

3. Click the **Print** button on the Print Preview toolbar to print the report; then close the document and exit Word.

You now have a hard copy of the EverRipe report including the table, which summarizes the report text. Brittany is pleased with your work.

Quick Check

1 Explain how to insert a blank table structure into a document.

2 How do you adjust the width of the columns in a table?

3 Why would you usually right-align numbers in a table?
   a. to quickly see the place value of the numbers
   b. to make the table look more attractive
   c. to make the table easier to understand
   d. all of the above

4 Define the following terms in your own words:
   a. table
   b. cell
   c. shading

5   List two ways to move from cell A1 to cell A2 in a table, then list two ways to move from cell B7 to cell B6.

6   Explain how to total a column of numbers in a table.

7   Explain how to insert a new row into a table.

In this tutorial, you have planned and formatted Brittany's recommendation report, and have added a table to summarize the report recommendations. As a result, the report information is readily available to readers who want to skim for the most important points, as well as to those who want more detailed information.

Tutorial Assignments

AgriTechnology adopted the recommendations the task force made in the EverRipe report. It is now two years later and the task force is issuing a report on the progress of the new packaging, distribution, and delivery policies. You'll format this report now.

1. If necessary, start Word and make sure your Student Disk is in the appropriate disk drive, and check your screen to make sure your settings match those in the tutorial. Display nonprinting characters as necessary

2. Open the file StatRep from the TAssign folder for Tutorial 3 on your Student Disk, and then save it as AgTech Status Report.

3. Divide the document into two sections. Insert a section break after the names of the task force members, and begin the executive summary on a new page.

4. Vertically align the first section of the document using the Justified alignment option in the Page Setup dialog box, and view the results in Print Preview.

5. Move the insertion point to section 2. Click View on the menu bar, and then click Header and Footer. Use the Word online Help system to learn the functions of the buttons on the Header and Footer toolbar. Then, on the Header and Footer toolbar, click the Switch Between Header and Footer button to move to the footer area of the document. Using the same techniques you used to create a header in the tutorial, create a footer for section 2 that reads "EverRipe Status Report" at the left margin, centers the page number preceded by the word "Page," and prints in 9-point bold Arial. (*Hint:* To center the page number, use the second tab stop.)

6. Create a header for this section that aligns your name at the left margin and the date at the right margin. (*Hint:* Use the Insert Date button on the Header and Footer toolbar to insert the date.) Close the Header and Footer toolbar.

7. Attach the Professional Report template to the document using the Style Gallery command on the Format menu, and preview how the report will look with sample text.

8. AutoFormat automatically formats selected text based on the options available in the attached template. Try using AutoFormat now by selecting the text of the title page, clicking Format on the menu bar, and then clicking AutoFormat on the Format menu. In the AutoFormat dialog box, make sure the AutoFormat now option button is selected, then click the OK button. Do you like the look of the formatted page? Why or why not?

9. Select the heading and text of the executive summary, and apply the Block Quotation style.

10. Apply the Heading 1 style to the heading "Introduction."

11. Apply the Heading 2 style to the headings "Loss of Profits for the EverRipe Crop," "Efforts to Improve Profitability," "Cost of the Improvements," and "Other Factors Influencing Profitability." Notice that the Heading 2 style does not insert space above the heading, so insert a return before each one.

12. Apply the Heading 3 style to the headings "Upgraded Packaging Plants," "Improved Distribution Methods," and "Improved Delivery." Insert a paragraph return before each Heading 3.

13. Save the document.

14. Preview and print the document, and then close it.

Open the file ZonReq from the TAssign folder for Tutorial 3 on your Student Disk, save the document as Zoning Request, and then complete the following:

15. Divide the document into two sections. End the first section after the words "Chicago, Illinois"; begin the second section on a new page.

16. Vertically align the first section of the document using the Top alignment option in the Page Setup dialog box.

17. Create a header for section 2 that prints "Zoning Request" at the left margin and has a right-aligned page number preceded by the word "Page."

18. On the Header and Footer toolbar, click the Switch Between Header and Footer button to move to the footer area of the document. Using the same techniques you used to create a header in the tutorial, create a footer for section 2 that aligns your name at the left margin and the date on the right margin.

19. Attach the Contemporary Report template to the document.

20. Using the styles you think most appropriate, format section 1. Preview the title page to make sure it fits on one page, and make any necessary adjustments.

21. Apply the Heading 1 style to the headings "Expansion Plans," "Benefits to the Community," and "Request for Zoning Changes." (*Hint:* After applying the style once, use the F4 key to apply it subsequent times.)

22. Apply the Heading 2 style to the headings "Plans to Expand Our Current Packaging Plant" and "Plans to Build a Distribution Center."

23. Apply the Block Quotation style to the "Summary" heading and paragraph text.

24. Save the document; then preview and print it.

Create a table before the Summary summarizing the Zoning Request report by completing the following:

25. Use the Insert Table button on the Standard toolbar to insert a 6-by-3 table. (In other words, a table with six rows and three columns.)

26. Type the headings "Project," "Cost" and "Jobs Added" in row 1.

27. In row 2, type "Expand Packaging Plant," "$1,200,000," and "150" in the appropriate cells.

28. In row 3, type "Build Distribution Center," "$1,300,000," and "150" in the appropriate cells.

29. Skip two rows, and then in the last row type "Total".

30. Use the AutoSum button on the Tables and Borders toolbar to total the Cost and Jobs Added column. Format the Cost total without decimal points using the Formula command on the Table menu.

31. Use the same techniques you learned for inserting rows to delete the blank row 4. Begin by selecting the row, and then right-clicking to open the Table shortcut menu. Then click Delete Rows. Repeat these steps to delete the remaining blank row.

32. Drag the right border of column B to the left until the border reaches 3 inches on the ruler. Drag the right border of column C (the Jobs Added column) to the left until the border reaches 4.25 inches on the ruler. Continue adjusting columns as necessary until the columns appear correctly formatted.

33. Right-align the numbers in the table and center the headings.

34. Format the heading row by adding a light gray shading and by bolding the headings as well. This time use the Tables and Borders toolbar. Click the Tables and Borders button to display the toolbar. Click the Shading Color arrow, and then click the light gray color of your choice.

35. Increase the height of the heading row, and then center the headings vertically in the row.

36. Center the table on the page by selecting all the table rows, and clicking the center button on the Formatting toolbar.

37. Preview, print and close the document.

Word will automatically convert text separated by commas, paragraph marks or tabs into a table. To try this feature now, open the file Members from the TAssign folder for Tutorial 3 on your Student Disk, and save it as Task Force Members. Then complete the following:

38. Select the list of task force members (including the heading), click Table on the menu bar, and then click Convert Text to Table. In the Convert Text to Table dialog box, make sure the settings indicate that the table should have 2 columns and that the text is currently separated by commas. Then click the OK button. Word automatically converts the list of task force members into a table.

39. Format the table appropriately, using the techniques you learned in the tutorial.

40. Save the document, and then preview and print it.

Case Problems

1. Ocean Breeze Bookstore Annual Report As manager of Ocean Breeze Bookstore in San Diego, California, Reed L. Paige must submit an annual report to the Board of Directors.

1. If necessary, start Word, make sure your Student Disk is in the appropriate drive, and check your screen to make sure your settings match those in the tutorials.

2. Open the file OceanRep from the Cases folder for Tutorial 3 on your Student Disk, and save it as Ocean Breeze Report. Then complete the following:

3. Divide the document into two sections. End the first section after the phrase "Ocean Breeze Bookstore"; begin section 2 on a new page.

 4. Move the insertion point to section 2. Create a header for the entire document that aligns "Ocean Breeze Annual Report" on the left margin and the date on the right margin. To make the header appear in both sections, select the Same as Previous button on the Header and Footer toolbar.

5. Attach the Elegant Report template to the document.

6. Apply the Part Label style to the title page text, and then vertically align the first section of the document using the Center alignment option in the Page Setup dialog box.

7. Select the heading and text of the summary and apply the Block Quotation style.

8. Apply the Heading 2 style to the headings "Introduction," "Mission Statement," "Company Philosophy," and "Organization." (*Hint:* Use the F4 key to apply the style the second and subsequent times.)

9. Apply the Heading 1 style to the headings "Children's Story Hour," "Summer Reading Contest," and "Home Delivery."

10. Apply the Heading 3 style to the headings "Board of Directors," "Store Management and Personnel," and "Autograph Signings."

11. Preview and save the document.

12. Scroll to the end of the document and insert one blank line. Then insert a 2-column by 8-row table listing first the members of the board of directors and then the managers. Use the headings "Name" and "Title." You'll find the names and titles listed in the report.

13. Adjust the table column widths as necessary.

14. Increase the height of the heading row, center the column headings horizontally and vertically, and then bold them.

15. Insert a row and add your name to the list of board of directors members.

 16. Format the heading row with a light gray shading.

17. Save, preview, print, and close the document.

2. Ultimate Travel's "Europe on a Budget" Report As director of Ultimate Travel's "Europe on a Budget" tour, Bronwyn Bates is required to write a report summarizing this year's tour.

1. If necessary, start Word, make sure your Student Disk is in the appropriate drive, and check your screen to make sure your settings match those in the tutorials.

2. Open the file Europe from the Cases folder for Tutorial 3 on your Student Disk, and save it as Europe Tour Report.

3. Divide the document into two sections. End the first section with the phrase "Tour Director"; begin the second section on a new page.

4. Vertically align the first section using the Center alignment option in the Page Setup dialog box.

5. Create a header for section 2 that contains the text "Ultimate Travel," centered. (*Hint:* To center text in the header, use the second tab stop.)

6. On the Header and Footer toolbar, click the Switch Between Header and Footer button to move to the footer area of the document. Using the same techniques you used to create a header in the tutorial, create a footer for section 2 that aligns "Evaluation Report" on the left margin and the date on the right margin.

7. Attach the Professional Report template to the document.

8. Apply the Heading 1 style to all the headings.

9. In the table, adjust column widths as necessary.

10. Bold the text in column A (the left-hand column) and then center it horizontally.

11. Use the same techniques you learned for inserting rows to delete the blank row 2: select the row, right-click to open the Table shortcut menu, and then click Delete Rows.

12. Format column A (the left-hand column) with a light gray shading.

13. Save, preview, print, and close the document.

3. Advisory Letter on a Tuition Increase Your school wants to raise tuition beginning next term. As head of the Student Advisory Board, you must submit a letter to the school's president about the increase.

1. If necessary, start Word, make sure your Student Disk is in the appropriate drive, and check your screen to make sure your settings match those in the tutorials.

2. Write a one-page letter explaining the following issues: what the current tuition or fees are at your school, what the new current tuition and fees will be, and three reasons why the school should wait for another year to increase tuition. Include a return address, inside address, date, salutation, and closing.

3. Save your document as Tuition Letter in the Cases folder for Tutorial 3 on your Student Disk.

4. Correct spelling and punctuation as necessary.

5. Attach the Professional Letter template.

EXPLORE

6. AutoFormat automatically formats selected text based on the options available in the attached template. Try using AutoFormat now by clicking Format on the menu bar, and then clicking AutoFormat. In the AutoFormat dialog box, click the AutoFormat and review each change option button, and then click the OK button. Do you like the look of the formatted letter? Why or why not? Accept the AutoFormat changes, or reject them and choose another format.

7. What are the font and paragraph attributes for the inside address and closing for the Professional Letter template? Apply new styles as necessary.

8. Print your letter.

9. Attach the Contemporary Letter template.

10. Use the Style list on the Formatting toolbar to apply new styles to each part of your letter.

11. Print your letter with the Contemporary Letter template styles.

12. Attach the Elegant Letter template.

13. What are the font and paragraph attributes for the date and body text for the Elegant Letter template?

14. Use either the Style list box or AutoFormat to apply new styles to each part of your letter.

15. Print your letter with the Elegant Letter template styles.

16. Save the current version of your letter using the filename Tuition Letter 2, and then close the document.

4. Monthly Menu Deciding what to cook each night can be difficult when it's dinnertime and you're hungry. To avoid making spaghetti every night next month, you'll plan next month's dinner menu now.

1. If necessary, start Word, make sure your Student Disk is in the appropriate drive, and check your screen to make sure your settings match those in the tutorials.

2. Open a new document and create a table (7 rows by 7 columns).

3. In row 2 of the table, type the days of the week in 12-point font of your choice.

4. Adjust the right column borders so that the name of each day of the week is on one line.

5. Bold the days of the week headings and center them horizontally in the cells. Add a light gray shading. Adjust column widths as necessary.

6. Type the number of each day of the month in a cell, and press the Enter key to place the number on its own line; then press the Tab key to move to the next cell. For example, if September 1 is a Tuesday, type "1" in cell C3, press the Enter key, and then press the Tab key. Repeat for the remaining days of the month.

7. Type the name of a main dish in the second line of each cell of the table for the first two weeks of the month.

8. Use a variation of drag and drop to copy each menu item from the first two weeks into the cells of the second two weeks. Highlight the first menu item (not including the date), and then press and hold down the Ctrl key and drag the menu item to the first day of the third week.

9. Fill in the remaining cells by copying menu items for the rest of the month.

10. Save the menu document as Monthly Menu in the Cases folder for Tutorial 3 on your Student Disk.

11. Preview and print the document. Then close the document.

Desktop Publishing a Newsletter

Creating a Newsletter for FastFad Manufacturing Company

CASE

FastFad Manufacturing Company

Gerrit Polansky works for FastFad Manufacturing Company, which designs and manufactures plastic figures (action figures, vehicles, and other toys) for promotional sales and giveaways in the fast-food and cereal industries. It is Gerrit's job to keep FastFad's sales staff informed about new products. He does this by producing and distributing a monthly newsletter that contains brief descriptions of these new items and ideas for marketing them. Recently, FastFad added MiniMovers, which are small plastic cars, trucks, and other vehicles, to its line of plastic toys. Gerrit needs to get the information about these products to the sales staff quickly—so the company can market the toys to FastFad's clients while the toys are still the fad. He has asked you to help him create the newsletter.

The newsletter needs to be eye-catching because the sales reps get a lot of printed product material and it's sometimes difficult for them to focus on any one product. Gerrit also wants you to create a newsletter that is neat, organized, and professional-looking. He wants it to contain headings so the sales reps can scan it quickly for the major points, as well as graphics that will give the newsletter a distinctive "look" that the reps will remember. He wants you to include a picture that will reinforce the newsletter content and help the reps remember the product. All of these tasks are easy in Word, especially with the Microsoft Clip Gallery, which lets you choose from a large collection of predesigned images that you can insert in your documents.

In this tutorial, you'll plan the layout of the newsletter, keeping in mind the audience (the sales representatives). Then you'll get acquainted with the desktop publishing features and elements you'll need to use to create the newsletter you want, and you'll learn how desktop publishing differs from other word processing tasks. You'll format the title using an eye-catching design and divide the document into newspaper-like columns to make it easier for the sales reps to read. You'll include a piece of predesigned art that adds interest and focus to the text. You'll then fine-tune the newsletter layout, give it a more professional appearance with typographic characters, and put a border around the page and a shaded background behind the text to give the newsletter a finished look.

SESSION

4.1

In this session, you will see how Gerrit planned his newsletter, and learn about desktop publishing features and elements. Then you will create the newsletter title using WordArt, modify the title's appearance, and then format the text of the newsletter into newspaper-style columns.

Planning the Document

The newsletter will provide a brief overview of the new FastFad products, followed by a short explanation of what the MiniMovers are and why children will like them. Like most newsletters, it will be written in an informal style that conveys information quickly. The newsletter title will be eye-catching and will help readers quickly identify the document. The newsletter text will be split into two columns to make it easier to read, and headings will help readers scan the information quickly. A picture will add interest and illustrate the newsletter content. Drop caps and other desktop publishing elements will help draw readers' attention to certain information, make the newsletter design attractive, and give it a professional appearance.

Features of Desktop Publishing

Desktop publishing is the production of commercial-quality printed material using a desktop computer system from which you can enter and edit text, create graphics, compose or lay out pages, and print documents. The following features are commonly associated with desktop publishing:

- **High-quality printing.** A laser printer or high-resolution inkjet printer produces high-quality final output.

- **Multiple fonts.** Two or three font types and sizes provide visual interest, guide the reader through the text, and convey the tone of the document.

- **Graphics.** Graphics, such as horizontal or vertical lines (called **rules**), boxes, electronic art, and digitized photographs help illustrate a concept or product, draw a reader's attention to the document, and make the text visually appealing.

- **Typographic characters.** Typographic characters such as typographic long dashes, called **em dashes** (—), in place of double hyphens (--) separate dependent clauses; typographic medium-width dashes, called **en dashes** (–), are used in place of hyphens (-) as minus signs and in ranges of numbers; and typographic bullets (•) signal items in a list to make the text professional-looking.

- **Columns and other formatting features.** Columns of text, **pull quotes** (small portions of text pulled out of the main text and enlarged), shaded areas and other special formatting features that you don't frequently see in letters and other documents distinguish desktop-published documents.

You'll incorporate many of these desktop publishing features into the FastFad newsletter for Gerrit.

Elements of a Desktop-Published Newsletter

Successful desktop publishing requires that you first know what elements professionals use to desktop publish a document. Figure 4-1 defines the desktop publishing elements that you have not yet used in the preceding tutorials. Gerrit wants you to incorporate these elements to produce the final copy of the newsletter shown in Figure 4-2. The newsletter includes some of the typical desktop publishing elements that you can add to a document using Word.

Figure 4-1 ◀
Desktop
publishing
elements

Element	Description
Columns	Two or more vertical blocks of text that fit on one page
WordArt	Text modified with special effects, such as rotated, curved, bent, shadowed, or shaded letters
Clip art	Prepared graphic images that are ready to be inserted into a document
Drop cap	Oversized first letter of word beginning a paragraph that extends vertically into two or more lines of the paragraph
Typographical symbols	Special characters that are not part of the standard keyboard, such as em dashes (—), copyright symbols (©), or curly quotation marks (")

Figure 4-2 ◀
FastFad
newsletter

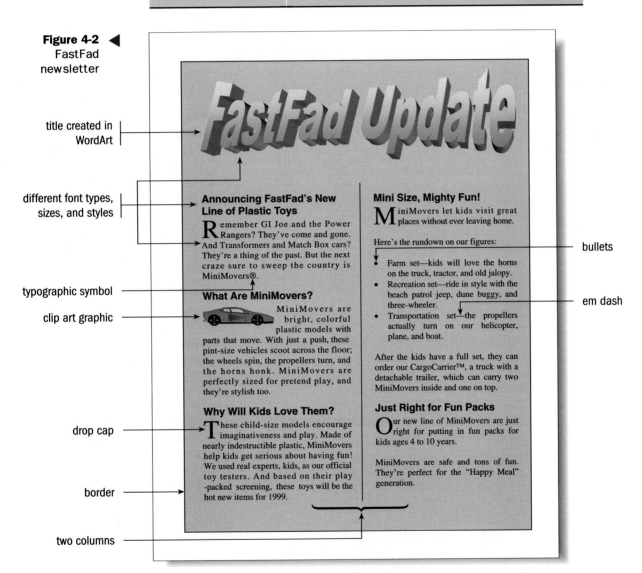

title created in WordArt

different font types, sizes, and styles

typographic symbol

clip art graphic

drop cap

border

two columns

bullets

em dash

Your first step is to create the newsletter's title.

Using WordArt to Create the Newsletter Title

Gerrit wants the title of the newsletter, "FastFad Update," to be eye-catching and dramatic, as shown in Figure 4-2. The Microsoft Office WordArt feature, available from Word as well as from other Microsoft Office 97 programs, provides great flexibility in designing text with special effects that expresses the image or mood you want to convey in your printed documents. With WordArt you can apply color and shading, as well as alter the shape and size of the text. You can easily "wrap" the document text around WordArt shapes.

You begin creating a WordArt image by choosing a text design from the WordArt Gallery. Then you type in the text you want to enhance, and format it.

When you create a WordArt image, Word automatically switches to page layout view. When the document is in normal view, WordArt images are not visible. Page layout view is the most appropriate view to use when you are desktop publishing with Word, because it shows you exactly how the text and graphics fit on the page, and the vertical ruler that appears in page layout view helps you to position graphical elements more precisely.

REFERENCE window

CREATING SPECIAL TEXT EFFECTS USING WORDART

- Click the Drawing button on the Standard toolbar to display the Drawing toolbar.
- Click the Insert WordArt button on the Drawing toolbar.
- Click the style of text you want to insert, and then click the OK button.
- Type the text you want in the Edit WordArt Text dialog box.
- Click the Font and Size list arrows to select the font and font size you want.
- If you want, click the Bold or Italic button, or both.
- Click the OK button.
- With the WordArt selected, drag any handle to reshape and resize it. To keep the text in the same proportions as the original, press and hold down the Shift key while you drag a handle.

To begin, you'll open the file that contains Gerrit's text, often called **copy**, and then you'll use WordArt to create the newsletter title. Gerrit wants the title formatted in the Arial font, since the headings in the rest of the document are in Arial.

To create the title of the newsletter using WordArt:

1. Start Word, and insert your Student Disk in the appropriate drive. Make sure your screen matches the figures in this tutorial, and make sure you display the nonprinting characters so you can see more accurately where to insert text and graphics.

2. Open the file **MiniInfo** from the **Tutorial.04** folder on your Student Disk, and then save it as **FastFad Newsletter**.

3. With the insertion point at the beginning of the document, press the **Enter** key to insert a new, blank line, and press the ↑ key to return the insertion point to the new, blank line. Then apply the **Normal** style using the Style list on the Formatting toolbar.

4. With the insertion point at the beginning of the document, click the **Drawing** button 🔲 on the Standard toolbar to display the Drawing toolbar, which appears at the bottom of the screen.

5. Click the **Insert WordArt** button 🔲 on the Drawing toolbar. The WordArt Gallery dialog box opens, displaying the 30 WordArt styles available.

6. Click the **WordArt style** in the bottom row, the fourth column from the left, as shown in Figure 4-3.

Figure 4-3 ◀
WordArt
Gallery styles

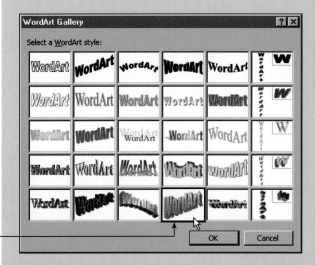

click this style ⎯⎯⎯⎯

7. Click the **OK** button. The Edit WordArt Text dialog box opens, displaying "Your Text Here," the default text, which you will replace with Gerrit's newsletter title.

8. Type **FastFad Update**. Make sure you make "FastFad" one word, no space.

9. Click the **OK** button.

The WordArt image appears as the newsletter title at the top of the newsletter, the WordArt toolbar appears on the screen, and the document changes to page layout view. Don't worry that the image partially covers the newsletter text or if it's below the first paragraph. You'll fix that later.

The WordArt image you have created is considered a Word **drawing object**. This means that you can modify its appearance (color, shape, size, alignment, etc.) using the buttons on the Drawing toolbar or the WordArt toolbar. Although the object looks like text, Word does not treat it like text. The object will not appear in normal view, and Word will not spell check it, as it does regular text. Think of it as a piece of art rather than as text.

The WordArt object is selected, indicated by the eight small squares called **resize handles** surrounding it, and the small yellow diamond called an **adjustment handle**. The resize and adjustment handles let you change the size and shape of the selected object. Before you change the size of the object, you'll first change its font size and formatting. The default font for this WordArt style is Impact, but Gerrit wants you to change it to match the font of the newsletter headings.

To change the font and formatting of the WordArt object:

1. Double-click the **WordArt object**. The Edit WordArt Text dialog box opens.

2. Click the Font list arrow, scroll to and then click **Arial Black**. The text in the preview box changes to Arial Black. Black indicates a thicker version of the Arial font, not its color. Now change the font size and style.

TROUBLE? If you do not have Arial Black on your font menu, choose Arial or another sans serif font.

3. Click the **Size** list arrow, scroll to and then click **40**, and then click the **Italic** button [*I*]. The text in the preview box enlarges to 40 points italic.

4. Click the **OK** button. The newsletter title changes to 40-point, italic Arial Black.

The default shape of the WordArt style you selected is an upward slanting shape called Cascade Up. Gerrit wants something a little more symmetrical. In WordArt, you can easily change the shape of any object to any of the 40 shapes that Word supplies.

To change the shape of the WordArt object:

1. Click the **WordArt Shape** button [⎚] on the WordArt toolbar. The palette of shapes appears, with the Cascade Up shape selected.

2. Click the **Deflate** shape (fourth row, second column from the left), as shown in Figure 4-4.

Figure 4-4 ◀
WordArt shapes

Deflate shape

WordArt toolbar

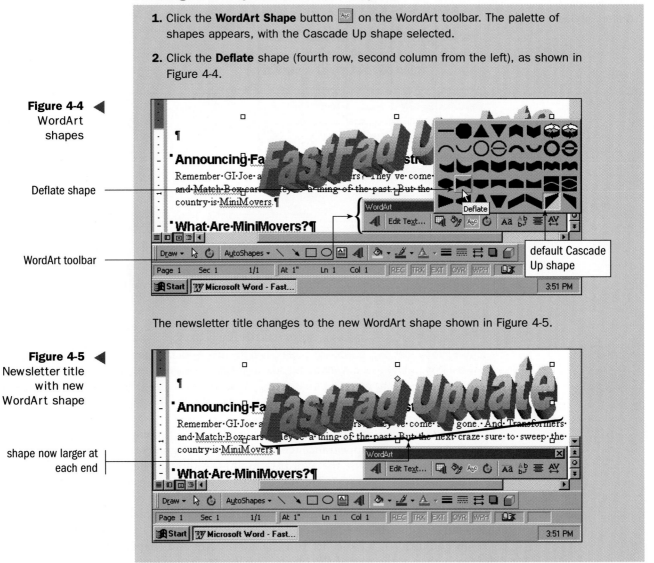

default Cascade Up shape

The newsletter title changes to the new WordArt shape shown in Figure 4-5.

Figure 4-5 ◀
Newsletter title with new WordArt shape

shape now larger at each end

Editing a WordArt Object

Now that the newsletter title is the font and shape you want, you'll move the title above the text and insert space between the WordArt object and the newsletter text. You'll do this using the text wrapping feature in the Format WordArt dialog box. This dialog box gives you the option of changing many WordArt features at once. For now, however, you'll just use it to separate the object from the text.

To insert space between the WordArt object and the newsletter text:

1. With the WordArt object selected, click the **Format WordArt** button 🖫 on the WordArt toolbar to open the Format WordArt dialog box.

2. Click the **Wrapping** tab.

3. In the Wrapping style section, click the **Top & bottom** icon. See Figure 4-6.

Figure 4-6 ◀
Settings to
separate
WordArt object
from text

Wrapping tab ──────

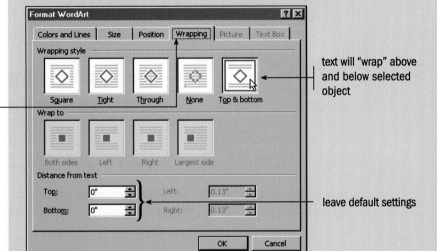

text will "wrap" above
and below selected
object

leave default settings

You could use the settings at the bottom of the dialog box to insert space between the object and the text, but the title object has enough space around it, so you don't need to change these settings now.

4. Click the **OK** button. The newsletter title is now above the text.

   TROUBLE? If the title is not above the text, drag it there now.

Now you only need to position the title and widen it proportionally so it fits neatly within the newsletter margins. The position of the WordArt object in the text is indicated by a small anchor symbol in the left margin. You can widen any WordArt object by dragging its resize handle. To keep the object the same proportion as the original, you hold down the Shift key as you drag the resize handle, which will prevent "stretching" the object more in one direction than the other. Then you'll rotate it a little so it looks more balanced.

To position, enlarge, and rotate the WordArt object:

1. Drag the WordArt object to the left until the lower-left corner of the first "F" in the word "FastFad" is aligned with the left margin and then release the mouse button. Since you can only see the text outline (not the text itself) as you drag the object, you might need to repeat the procedure. Use the left edge of the text or the left margin in the ruler as a guide.

2. With the WordArt object still selected, position the pointer over its lower-right resize handle. The pointer changes to ↘.

3. Press and hold the **Shift** key and drag the resize handle to the right margin, using the horizontal ruler as a guide. See Figure 4-7. As you drag the handle, the pointer changes to ✛. If necessary, repeat the procedure to make the rightmost edge of the "e" in the word "Update" line up with the right margin. Now you'll lower the right side of the WordArt object.

Figure 4-7 ◀
Resizing the
WordArt object

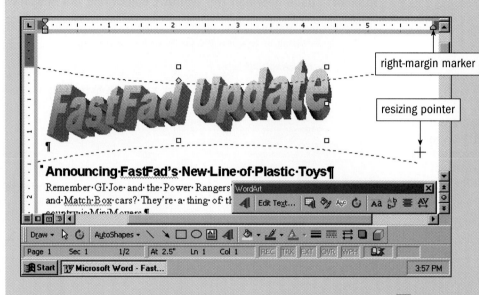

right-margin marker

resizing pointer

4. With the WordArt object still selected, click the **Free Rotate** button ⟳ on the WordArt toolbar. Small green rotation handles surround the object.

5. Move the pointer over the document. The pointer changes to ⟲.

6. Position the pointer over the green circle on the lower-right corner of the object, and then drag the rotation handle down about a half inch, or until the title text appears to be horizontal. See Figure 4-8.

Figure 4-8 ◀
Rotating the
WordArt Object

lower the right side of
the image

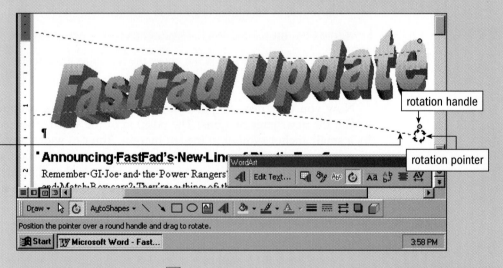

rotation handle

rotation pointer

7. Click the **Drawing** button 🖾 on the Standard toolbar to close the Drawing toolbar, and then click anywhere in the newsletter text to deselect the WordArt object. See Figure 4-9.

Word

Figure 4-9
Newsletter
after enlarging
and rotating
the WordArt
object

title aligned between
left and right margins

You have inserted and formatted a WordArt object that will draw the attention of the sales reps to the newsletter as they review this document among all the other product literature they have to read.

Formatting Text into Newspaper-Style Columns

Because newsletters are meant for quick reading, they usually are laid out in newspaper-style columns. In **newspaper-style columns**, a page is divided into two or more vertical blocks or columns. Text flows down one column, continues at the top of the next column, flows down that column, and so forth. Newspaper-style columns are easier to read because the columns tend to be narrow and the type size a bit smaller than the text in a letter. This enables the eye to see more text in one glance than when text is set in longer line lengths and in a larger font size.

If you want some of your text to be in columns and other text to be in full line lengths, you must insert section breaks into your document and apply the column format only to those sections you want in columns. In this case, Gerrit wants only the text below the title to be divided into two columns. You could select this text and use the Columns button on the Standard toolbar to automatically insert a section break and divide the text into columns, but Gerrit also wants you to add a vertical line between the columns. So you'll use the Columns command on the Format menu, which lets you both divide the text into columns with a line between them and insert a section break in the location you specify. Without the section break, the line between the columns would extend up through the title.

FORMATTING TEXT INTO NEWSPAPER-STYLE COLUMNS

- Select the text you want to divide into columns, or don't select any text if you want the entire document divided into columns.
- Click the Columns button on the Standard toolbar, and highlight the number of columns you want to divide the text into.
  or
- Move the insertion point to the location where you want the columns to begin.
- Click Format on the menu bar, and then click Columns to open the Columns dialog box.
- Select the column style in the Presets section, and type the number of columns you want in the Number of columns text box.
- If necessary, click the Equal column width check box to deselect it, and then set the width of each column in the Width and spacing section.
- Click the Apply to list arrow, and select the This point forward or Whole document option.
- If you want a vertical rule between the columns, click the Line between check box and click the OK button.

To apply newspaper-style columns to the body of the newsletter:

1. Position the insertion point to the left of the word "Announcing" just below the title.

2. Click **Format** on the menu bar, and then click **Columns**. The Columns dialog box opens.

3. In the Presets section, click the **Two** icon.

4. If necessary, click the **Line between** check box to select it. The text in the Preview box changes to a two-column format with a vertical rule between the columns.

You want these changes to affect only the text after the title, so you'll need to insert a section break and apply the column formatting to the text after the insertion point.

5. Click the **Apply to** list arrow, and then click **This point forward** to have Word automatically insert a section break at the insertion point. See Figure 4-10.

Figure 4-10 ◀
Completed columns dialog box

creates two columns of the same width

adds section break at insertion point location

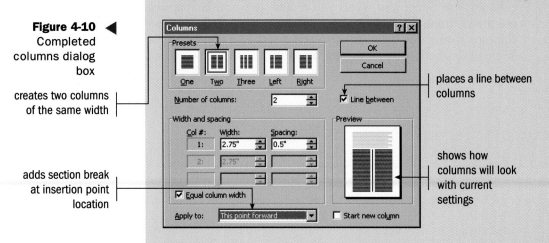

places a line between columns

shows how columns will look with current settings

6. Click the **OK** button to close the dialog box and return to the document window. A section break appears, and the insertion point is now positioned in section 2.

TROUBLE? You might need to move the WordArt object so it is above the section break. If necessary, drag the WordArt object above the section break. The section break moves down and the two-column text begins just after it. If necessary, drag the WordArt object again to adjust its position. When an object is selected, you can also use the arrow keys on the keyboard to adjust its position.

7. Click anywhere in the newsletter text to deselect the WordArt object.

Viewing the Whole Page

As you lay out a document for desktop publishing, you should periodically look at the whole page, so you can see how the layout looks. The best way to do this is in page layout view using Zoom Control.

To zoom out and view the whole page:

1. Click the **Zoom Control** list arrow ⌊100% ▾⌋ on the Standard toolbar, and then click **Whole Page**. Word displays the entire page of the newsletter so you can see how the two-column format looks on the page. See Figure 4-11.

Figure 4-11 ◀
Page layout view showing the two columns

section break between title and copy

line between columns

text arranged in two columns

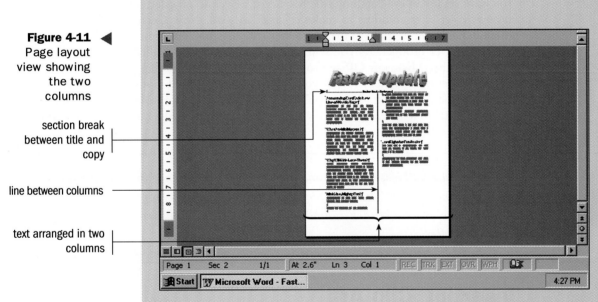

TROUBLE? Your columns may break at a slightly different line than those shown in the figure. This is not a problem; just continue with the tutorial.

The newsletter title, now with a horizontal orientation, is centered on the page and the copy is in a two-column format. The text fills the left column but not the right column, and the top of the right column is higher than the left. You'll fix this later, after you add a graphic and format some of the text.

2. Click the **Zoom Control** list arrow again, and then click **100%**. Word returns to the full-size page layout view.

3. Save the document.

Quick Check

[1] In your own words, explain three features commonly associated with desktop publishing.

2 In your own words, define the following terms:
  a. WordArt
  b. resize handle
  c. newspaper-style columns

3 List the steps for creating a WordArt object in a Word document.

4 How do you change the size of a WordArt object after you have inserted it into a Word document?

5 What is the purpose of the WordArt Shape button on the WordArt toolbar?

6 True or False: Normal view shows how text will fit into newspaper-style columns.

7 To format text into newspaper-like columns, you use the _____ command on the _____ menu.

8 If you want one part of your document to be in two columns and another part to be in full width, you must insert a _____ between the two sections.

9 True or False: Formatting a document into newspaper-like columns will automatically make the columns of equal length.

You have set up an eye-catching title for Gerrit's FastFad newsletter and formatted the text in newspaper style columns to make it easier to read. Now Gerrit wants you to insert a graphic that is appropriate to the newsletter content, possibly some type of car to represent the MiniMover product. As you will see, the Microsoft Clip Gallery, available from Word as well as other Microsoft Office programs, contains graphics that you can use with many different types of documents. After you add clip art, you'll add more graphic interest by formatting some of the text. Then you'll give the newsletter a finished look by making the columns equal in length, and give the page some depth by adding a shaded background.

SESSION 4.2

In this session you will insert, resize, and crop clip art, and change the way the text wraps around the clip art. Then you'll create drop caps, insert typographic symbols, balance columns, place a border around the newsletter, add a shaded background, and print the newsletter.

Inserting Clip Art

Graphics, which can include artwork, photographs, charts, tables, designs, or even designed text like WordArt, add variety to documents and are especially appropriate for newsletters. Word enables you to include many types of graphics in your documents. You can create a graphic in another Windows program and insert it into your document using the Picture command on the Insert menu. You can also insert a picture, as well as sounds and videos, from the Microsoft Clip Gallery, a collection of **clip art** images, or existing artwork that you can insert into documents, which is part of Microsoft Office 97. You will insert an existing piece of clip art into the newsletter. Gerrit wants you to use a graphic that reflects the newsletter content.

INSERTING CLIP ART

- Move the insertion point to the location in your document where you want the graphic image to appear.
- Click Insert on the menu bar, point to Picture, and then click Clip Art to open the Microsoft Clip Gallery 3.0 dialog box.
- Click the Clip Art tab.
- Click the category that best represents the type of art you need.
- Click the image you want to use.
- Click the Insert button.

To insert the clip art image of a car into the newsletter:

1. If you took a break after the last session, make sure Word is running, the FastFad Newsletter is open, the document is in page layout view, and the non-printing characters are displayed.

2. Position the insertion point to the left of the word "MiniMovers" in the second paragraph of the newsletter just below the heading.

3. Click **Insert** on the menu bar, point to **Picture**, and then click **Clip Art**. The Microsoft Clip Gallery 3.0 dialog box opens.

   TROUBLE? If you see a dialog box informing you that additional clips are available on the Microsoft Office CD-ROM, click the OK button.

4. If necessary, click the **Clip Art** tab to display the clip art options, and then click the **Transportation** category.

5. Click the **red sports car image** in the upper-left corner of the preview window. See Figure 4-12.

Figure 4-12 ◀
Clip Art tab of
the Microsoft
Clip Gallery 3.0
dialog box

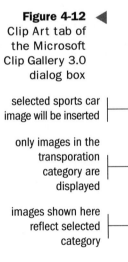

selected sports car image will be inserted

only images in the transporation category are displayed

images shown here reflect selected category

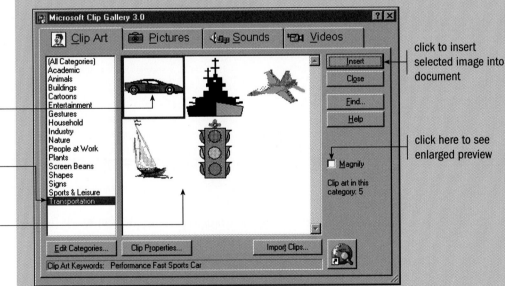

click to insert selected image into document

click here to see enlarged preview

6. Click the **Insert** button to insert the image of the red sports car in the newsletter at the insertion point, and then save the newsletter.

   The sports car clip art extends across both columns. Like the WordArt object you worked with earlier, the clip art image is a graphic object with resize handles that you can use to change its size. Word inserts an anchor symbol in the left margin, indicating the object's position relative to the text. The Picture toolbar appears whenever the clip art object is selected. See Figure 4-13.

Figure 4-13 ◀
The newsletter
with the clip art
object inserted

resize handles

object inserted at
insertion point
between heading
and text

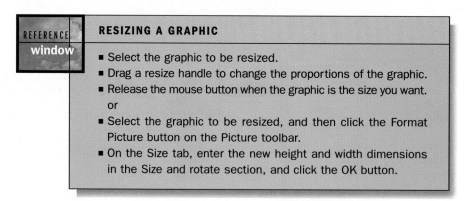

TROUBLE? If your graphic object does not extend into the second column, just continue with the tutorial.

Gerrit would like the image to be smaller so it doesn't distract attention from the text.

Resizing a Graphic

Often, you need to change the size of a graphic so that it fits into your document better. This is called **scaling** the image. You can resize a graphic by either dragging its resize handles or, for more precise control, by using the Format Picture dialog box.

REFERENCE
window

RESIZING A GRAPHIC

- Select the graphic to be resized.
- Drag a resize handle to change the proportions of the graphic.
- Release the mouse button when the graphic is the size you want.
or
- Select the graphic to be resized, and then click the Format Picture button on the Picture toolbar.
- On the Size tab, enter the new height and width dimensions in the Size and rotate section, and click the OK button.

For Gerrit's newsletter, the dragging technique will work fine.

To resize the clip art graphic:

1. Make sure the clip art graphic is selected, and scroll to the right so you can see the lower-right resize handle of the object.

2. Drag the lower-right resize handle up and to the left, so the front of the car extends only about halfway into the first column. You don't have to hold down the Shift key, as you do with WordArt, to resize it proportionally. See Figure 4-14.

Figure 4-14 ◀
Resizing the
sports car
graphic

anchor symbol
indicates position
relative to text

dotted line box
indicates new size

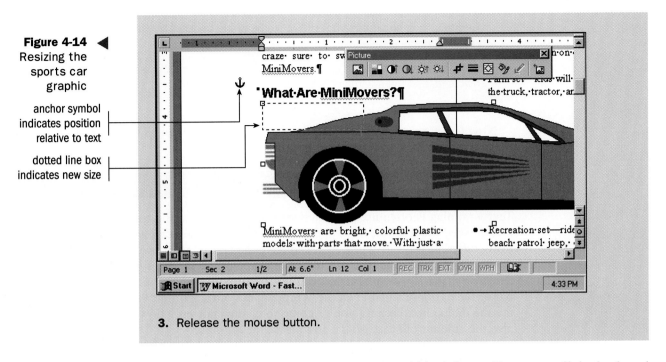

3. Release the mouse button.

Gerrit wonders if the sports car image would look better if you cut off the back end and showed only the front half.

Cropping a Graphic

You can **crop** the graphic, that is, cut off one or more of its edges, using either the Crop button on the Picture toolbar or the Format Picture dialog box. Once you crop a graphic, the part you crop off becomes hidden from view, but still remains a part of the graphic image, so you can always change your mind and restore a cropped graphic to it original form.

To crop the sports car graphic:

1. If necessary, click the clip art to select it. The resize handles appear.

2. Click the **Crop** button ⊞ on the Picture toolbar.

3. Position the pointer directly over the left-middle resize handle of the object. The pointer changes to ⇱ .

4. Press and hold down the mouse button and drag the handle to the right so that only the front door and hood are visible. and then release the mouse button. See Figure 4-15.

Figure 4-15 ◀
Cropping the
sports car
graphic

cropping tool

left half of image
hidden from view

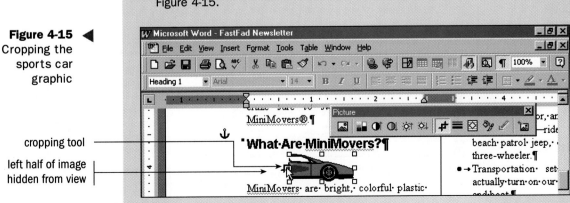

Gerrit decides he prefers you to display the whole sports car, so he asks you to return to the original image.

5. Click the **Undo** button 🔄 on the Standard toolbar. The cropping action is reversed, and the full image of the sports car reappears.

Now Gerrit wants you to make the text to wrap (or flow) to the right of the graphic, making the car look as if it's driving into the text.

Wrapping Text Around a Graphic

Text wrapping is often used in newsletters to add interest and to prevent excessive open areas, called **white space**, from appearing on the page. You can wrap text around objects many different ways in Word. You can have the text wrap above and below the graphic, through it, or wrap the text to follow the shape of the object, even if the graphic has an irregular shape. To wrap text you can use the Text Wrapping button on the Picture toolbar or the options available on the Wrapping tab of the Format Picture dialog box. You'll use the dialog box because you're going to change not only how the text will wrap, but also the amount of space above and below the graphic.

To wrap text around the car graphic:

1. If necessary, click the clip art to select it.

2. Click the **Format Picture** button 🖼️ on the Picture toolbar. The Format Picture dialog box opens.

3. Click the **Wrapping** tab.

4. In the Wrapping style section, click the **Tight** icon, the second icon from the left.

5. In the Wrap to section, click the **Right** icon.

6. In the Distance from text section, click the **Right** up arrow once to display **.2"**. Don't worry about the Left setting, since the text will wrap only around the right side. Now you'll add space above the graphic so it is separated from the section heading.

7. Click the **Position** tab, and click the **Vertical** arrows until the text box displays **.5"**.

8. Click the **OK** button. The text wraps around the car, following its shape.

9. Click anywhere in the text to deselect the graphic, and then save the newsletter. Your screen should look similar to Figure 4-16.

Figure 4-16 ◀
Text wrapped
around graphic

graphic separated
from text above
and below

text fits around
irregular shape

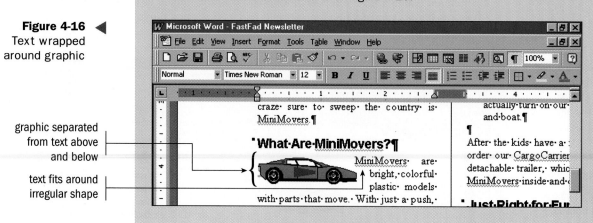

The image of the sports car draws the reader's attention to the beginning of the newsletter, but the rest of the text looks somewhat plain. Gerrit suggests adding a drop cap at the beginning of each section.

Inserting Drop Caps

A **drop cap** is a large, uppercase (capital) letter that highlights the beginning of the text of a newsletter, chapter, or some other document section. The drop cap usually extends from the top of the first line of the paragraph down two or three succeeding lines of the paragraph. The text of the paragraph wraps around the drop cap. Word allows you to create a drop cap for the first letter of the first word of a paragraph.

You will create a drop cap for the first paragraph following each heading in the newsletter (except for the first heading, where the clip art image is located). The drop cap will extend two lines into the paragraph.

INSERTING DROP CAPS

- Position the insertion point in the paragraph for which you want to create a drop cap.
- Click Format on the menu bar, and then click Drop Cap to open the Drop Cap dialog box.
- In the Position section, click the icon for the type of drop cap you want: Dropped or In Margin.
- Click the Font list arrow, and select the font you want for the drop cap.
- Set the appropriate number in the Lines to drop text box.
- If necessary, enter a new value for the Distance from text option and click the OK button.

To insert drop caps in the newsletter:

1. Position the insertion point in the paragraph following the first heading, just to the left of the word "Remember."

2. Click **Format** on the menu bar, and then click **Drop Cap**. The Drop Cap dialog box opens.

3. In the Position section, click the **Dropped** icon.

4. Click the **Lines to drop** down arrow once to display **2**. You won't need to change the default distance from the text. See Figure 4-17.

Figure 4-17 ◄
Drop Cap
dialog box

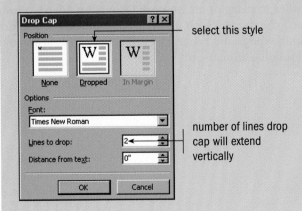

select this style

number of lines drop
cap will extend
vertically

5. Click the **OK** button to close the dialog box. Word automatically formats the first character of the paragraph as a drop cap. See Figure 4-18.

Figure 4-18 ◄
Drop cap
begins the
paragraph

text wraps around
drop cap

drop cap selected

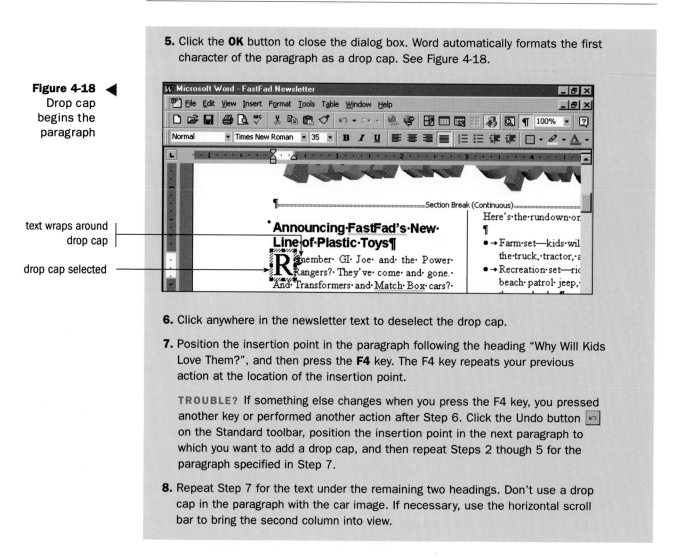

6. Click anywhere in the newsletter text to deselect the drop cap.

7. Position the insertion point in the paragraph following the heading "Why Will Kids Love Them?", and then press the **F4** key. The F4 key repeats your previous action at the location of the insertion point.

   TROUBLE? If something else changes when you press the F4 key, you pressed another key or performed another action after Step 6. Click the Undo button on the Standard toolbar, position the insertion point in the next paragraph to which you want to add a drop cap, and then repeat Steps 2 though 5 for the paragraph specified in Step 7.

8. Repeat Step 7 for the text under the remaining two headings. Don't use a drop cap in the paragraph with the car image. If necessary, use the horizontal scroll bar to bring the second column into view.

The newsletter looks more lively with the drop caps. Next, you turn your attention to the issue of inserting a registered trademark symbol beside the trademark names.

Inserting Symbols and Special Characters

Gerrit used standard word-processing characters rather than **typographic characters** (special symbols and punctuation marks) when he typed the newsletter copy. For example, he typed straight quotation marks instead of curly quotation marks and he typed two dashes in place of an em dash. However, Word automatically converted some of the standard characters (such as the dashes and the quotation marks) into the more polished looking typographic characters. Figure 4-19 lists some the characters that Word converts to symbols automatically.

Figure 4-19 ◀
Common
typographical
symbols

To insert this symbol or character	Type	Word converts it to
em dash	word- -word	word—word
quotation marks	"word"	"word"
copyright symbol	(c)	©
registered trademark symbol	(r)	®
trademark symbol	(tm)	™
ordinal numbers	1st, 2nd, 3rd, etc.	1st, 2nd, 3rd, etc.
fractions	1/2, 1/4	½, ¼
arrows	--> or <--	→ or ←

To insert typographic characters into a finished document after you've finished typing it, it's easiest to use the Symbol command on the Insert menu. In order to make the newsletter look professionally formatted, you'll insert a special character now—namely, a registered trademark symbol—at the appropriate places.

FastFad protects the names of its products by registering the names as trademarks. You'll indicate that in the newsletter by inserting the registered trademark symbol (®) at the first occurrence of the trademark names "MiniMovers" and a trademark symbol (™) for the first occurrence of "CargoCarrier."

REFERENCE window

INSERTING SYMBOLS AND SPECIAL CHARACTERS

- Move the insertion point to the location where you want to insert a particular symbol or special character.
- Click Insert on the menu bar, and then click Symbol to open the Symbol dialog box.
- Click the appropriate symbol from those shown in the symbol character set on the Symbols tab, or click the name from the list on the Special Characters tab.
- Click the Insert button.
- Click the Close button.

To insert the registered trademark symbol:

1. Position the insertion point at the end of the word "MiniMovers" in the first paragraph, just before the period.

2. Click **Insert** on the menu bar, and then click **Symbol** to open the Symbol dialog box.

3. If necessary, click the **Special Characters** tab. See Figure 4-20.

Figure 4-20
Special
Characters tab
in Symbol
dialog box

click to display
this tab

insert this symbol

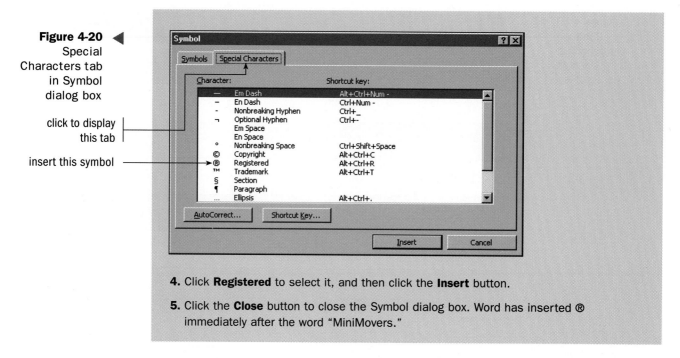

4. Click **Registered** to select it, and then click the **Insert** button.

5. Click the **Close** button to close the Symbol dialog box. Word has inserted ® immediately after the word "MiniMovers."

If you have to insert symbols repeatedly, or if you want to insert them quickly as you type, it's often easier to use the Word AutoCorrect feature to insert them. You'll use AutoCorrect now to insert the trademark symbol (™) after the first occurrence of CargoCarrier. First, you'll look in the AutoCorrect settings to make sure the correct entry is there.

To enter a symbol using AutoCorrect:

1. Click **Tools** on the menu bar, and then click **AutoCorrect**. In the Replace column on the left side of the dialog box, you see (tm), which means that any occurrence of (tm) in the document will automatically be corrected to the trademark symbol.

2. Click the **Cancel** button.

3. Position the insertion point just after the word "CargoCarrier" in the second column, in the paragraph above the heading "Just Right for Fun Packs."

4. Type **(tm)**. Word automatically converts your typed characters into the trademark symbol.

The trademark symbols help make the newsletter look more professional. Next, you decide to adjust the columns of text so they are approximately the same length.

Balancing the Columns

You could shift text from one column to another by adding blank paragraphs to move the text into the next column or by deleting blank paragraphs to shorten the text so it will fit into one column. Instead, Word can automatically **balance** the columns, or make them of equal length, for you.

To balance the columns:

1. Position the insertion point at the end of the text in the right column, just after period following the word "generation." Now change the zoom control to Whole Page so you can see the full effect of the change.

2. Click the **Zoom Control** list arrow on the Standard toolbar, and then click **Whole Page**.

3. Click **Insert** on the menu bar, and then click **Break**. The Break dialog box opens.

4. In the Section breaks section, click the **Continuous** option button.

5. Click the **OK** button. Word inserts a continuous section break at the end of the text, which, along with the first section break you inserted earlier, defines the area in which it should balance the columns.

As you can see, Word automatically balances the text between the two section breaks.

The balanced columns make the layout look much more professional. However, notice that the top margin is narrower than the bottom margin. The newsletter would look better if it had the same amount of space above and below the content. You can do this by enlarging the document's top margin.

To increase the top margin of the newsletter:

1. Click **File** on the menu bar, and then click **Page Setup**. The Page Setup dialog box opens.

2. If necessary, click the **Margins** tab to select it.

3. Click the **Top** up arrow four times to increase the setting to **1.4"**.

4. In the **Apply to** list box in the lower-right portion of the dialog box, select **Whole Document**.

5. Click the **OK** button. The entire content of the newsletter moves down, creating a similar amount of space above and below it. See Figure 4-21.

Figure 4-21 ◀
The newsletter with balanced columns and vertical placement

columns now of equal length

top and bottom margins are the same

TROUBLE? Depending on the size of the WordArt object, the placement of your newsletter content may differ from that shown in the figure. Adjust the size of the WordArt object and the top margin until the newsletter is centered vertically on the page.

Drawing a Border Around the Page

Gerrit wants to give the newsletter a little more pizzazz. He suggests adding a border around the newsletter, and adding a shaded background. In the steps that follow, you'll create a page border and background using the Word Drawing toolbar. You'll also learn how to move an object—in this case, a shaded box—behind text and other objects. In the Tutorial Assignments, you'll learn how to insert a page border using another, more automated method—the Page Border command.

To draw a border around the newsletter:

1. Make sure the document is in page layout view and that the zoom control setting is set to Whole Page, so you can see the entire newsletter.

2. Click the **Drawing** button 🖎 on the Standard toolbar. The Drawing toolbar appears at the bottom of the document window.

3. Click the **Rectangle** button 🔲 on the Drawing toolbar.

4. Position the pointer slightly higher than and to the left of the first "F" in the "FastFad" title near the upper-left corner of the newsletter. The pointer changes to ＋ when positioned over the document.

5. Click and drag the pointer to the lower-right corner of the newsletter to surround the newsletter with a box. See Figure 4-22.

Figure 4-22 ◀
Drawing a border around the newsletter

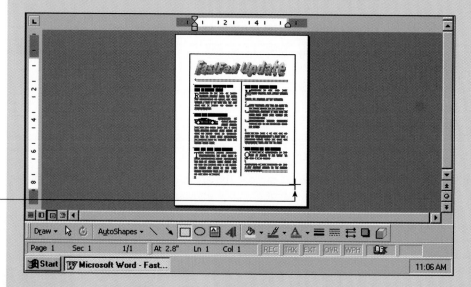

drawing pointer —

6. Release the mouse button.

When you release the mouse button, a white rectangle covers the newsletter text. You'll fix this in a minute.

7. Click the **Line Style** button ☰ on the Drawing toolbar to display a list of line style options. See Figure 4-23.

Figure 4-23 ◀
Line styles on the Drawing toolbar

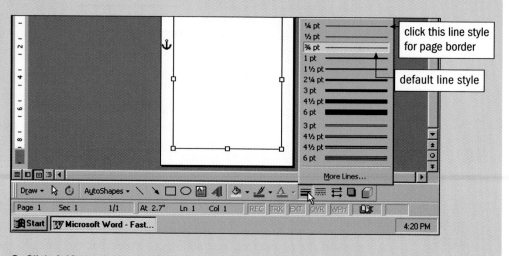

click this line style for page border

default line style

8. Click **1/4 pt** at the top of the list to select this line style option.

Word

9. Click the list arrow next to the **Fill Color** button 🎨 on the Drawing toolbar, and then click More Fill Colors to open the Colors dialog box. Here you can select or customize the color you want for the shaded background.

10. Click the **first gray color tile** in the second row from the bottom. A preview of the color you have selected appears in the top half of the preview square on the right side of the dialog box. See Figure 4-24.

Figure 4-24 ◀
Selecting a
fill color

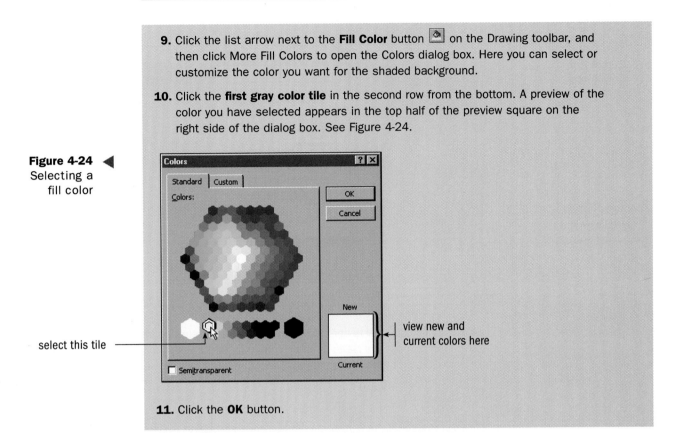

select this tile ——

view new and
current colors here

11. Click the **OK** button.

The fill color covers the text, but you want it to be a background shading. You'll need to send the filled rectangle to the back or bring the text to the front in order to see the text over the fill, which you'll do in the next section.

Document Layers

When you add shading or lines around text, you are creating layers. Think of printing your document on two sheets of clear plastic. One sheet contains the text of your document, the other sheet contains borders and shading. When you place one sheet on top of the other, or layer them, the sheets' contents combine to create the complete document. If you place the sheet with shading and borders over the text, you cannot see the text through it. If you place the sheet with the text over the shading and borders, the shading and borders are visible around the text.

Right now the background shading is positioned as the top layer of the document. You need to send that layer to the back of the text layer so the shading is visible behind the text instead of obscuring it.

To move the shading to the back and print the final newsletter:

1. Click the **Draw** button on the Drawing toolbar.

2. Point to **Order**, and then click **Send to Back**. The shaded box moves to the layer behind the WordArt and ClipArt objects.

3. Click the **Draw** button again, point to **Order**, and then click **Send Behind Text**. The shaded box moves to the layer behind the text.

4. Click anywhere in the newsletter text to deselect the border. The text layer and the graphics appear on top of the shading layer. See Figure 4-25.

Figure 4-25 ◀
Completed
newsletter

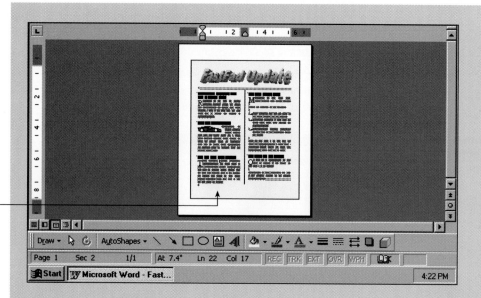

filled rectangle is now
behind newsletter
copy and graphics

TROUBLE? If the sports car disappears from the newsletter, you selected Send Behind Text, instead of Send to Back in Step 2. To correct this, select the shaded rectangle, and then repeat Steps 1 and 2, making sure you select Send to Back from the Order menu.

5. Save the completed newsletter.

6. Click the **Print Preview** button on the Standard toolbar. Preview the newsletter.

7. Click the **Print** button on the Print Preview toolbar to print the newsletter. If you have a black-and-white printer, the orange and yellow letters of the title and the red car appear in shades of gray.

TROUBLE? If you see an error message when you try to print, your printer might not have enough memory to print the newsletter with the background shading. Return to page layout view. Click the border to select it, click the Fill Color list arrow on the Drawing toolbar, click No Fill as the color to remove the background shading, and then try to print again. If you still have problems, ask your instructor or technical support person for assistance.

8. If necessary, click the **Close** button on the Print Preview toolbar to return to page layout view.

9. Close the newsletter and exit Word.

Quick **Check**

1. Define the following in your own words:
   a. clip art
   b. typographic characters
   c. drop cap
   d. crop

2. Describe the procedure for inserting a clip art graphic in Word.

3. In your own words, explain the difference between resizing and cropping a graphic.

4. Describe the procedure for creating a drop cap.

5. How do you insert the registered trademark symbol in a document? What are two other symbols or special characters that you can add to a document with Word?

6 Besides the Symbol command on the Insert menu, what is another way of entering typographic symbols?

7 Describe the process for drawing a border around text and adding background shading.

8 Describe the procedure for balancing columns in Word.

You give the printed newsletter to Gerrit, along with a copy on disk. He thinks it looks great and thanks you for your help. He'll print it later on a color printer (in order to make the most of the colors in the WordArt title and the sports car clip art) and distribute the newsletter to FastFad's sales staff.

Tutorial Assignments

Gerrit's FastFad newsletter was a success; the sales representatives all seemed to have good product knowledge, and the sales for MiniMovers were brisk. The sales reps themselves have asked Gerrit for a product information sheet, similar to the newsletter, about another product, FastFad Sports Figures. The sales reps want to be able to print it and send it directly to their clients. You'll produce that newsletter now.

1. If necessary, start Word and make sure your Student Disk is in the appropriate disk drive. Check your screen to make sure your settings match those in the tutorial and that the nonprinting characters and Drawing toolbar are displayed.

2. Open the file FigSpecs from the TAssign folder for Tutorial 4 on your Student Disk, and then save it as Sports Figures.

3. Insert a new, blank line at the top of the document, format in Normal style, and then click the Insert WordArt button on the Drawing toolbar.

4. Choose the WordArt style in the lower-left corner of the WordArt Gallery dialog box.

5. Type "FastFad Figures" in the Enter WordArt Text dialog box, click OK, and then drag the WordArt above the first heading.

6. Use the WordArt Shape button on the WordArt toolbar to apply the Deflate shape (fourth row, second column from left), and change the font to 24 point Arial bold.

7. Use the Format WordArt dialog box Wrapping tab to apply the Top & bottom wrapping style.

8. Drag the lower-right and then the lower-left resize handles to enlarge the image to the entire width between the left and right margins.

9. Save the document.

10. Position the insertion point to the left of the first word in the first heading, and then format the text into two columns using the Columns dialog box. Insert a section break so that the columns appear from this point forward. Do not insert a line between columns.

11. View the whole newsletter in page layout view, using the Whole Page zoom control setting, and make any necessary adjustments.

12. Return to 100% zoom control in page layout view, and then position the insertion point immediately after the first paragraph (on the same line). Click Insert on the menu bar, point to Picture, and then click **Clip Art** to open the Microsoft Clip Gallery dialog box.

13. Insert the tennis player clip art image from the Sports & Leisure category.

14. Select and resize the sports image so it fits in the left half of the first column.

15. Crop the graphic to remove the tennis racket from the left side of the image, and then move the graphic left using the keyboard arrow keys.

16. Select the clip art object, click the Format Picture button on the Picture toolbar, and click the Wrapping tab. Set the Wrapping style to Tight, and wrap the text around the right side of the image for the Dropped position.

17. Format a drop cap for the first paragraph following the "Five Sets of Figures" heading, using the default settings for the Dropped position.

18. Insert the trademark symbol after the first occurrence of "FastFad Sports Figures," using either of the techniques you used in the tutorial.

19. As you might have noticed, Word automatically justifies text in newspaper columns. To try changing the alignment now: Select both columns of text by clicking before the first word of text, pressing and holding down the Shift key, and then clicking at the end of the text. Use the Align Left button on the Formatting toolbar to change the columns' text alignment to left alignment.

20. Make the columns of equal length by balancing the columns. Position the insertion point at the end of the document, click Insert on the menu bar, and then click Break. In the Section breaks section, click the Continuous option button, and then click the OK button.

21. A pull quote is a phrase or quotation taken from the text that summarizes a key point. To insert a pull quote now: Select the words "FastFad: We take play seriously" (at the end of the second column) and then click the Cut button on the Standard toolbar. Click the Text Box button on the Drawing toolbar, and then below the two columns, drag the pointer to draw a text box that spans the width of the page. With the insertion point located in the text box, click the Paste button on the Standard toolbar. Select the text in the text box, and then use the Font command on the Format menu to format the text in the box as 16 point Arial italic. Click the Center button on the Formatting toolbar to center the text in the box. Use the Fill Color list arrow on the Drawing toolbar to fill the selected text box with a light turquoise color.

22. Sometimes you may want to use the Replace command to replace standard word processing characters with typographic characters. To replace every occurrence of -- (two dashes) with — (em dash): Position the insertion point at the beginning of the first paragraph of text. Click Edit on the menu bar, and then click Replace. In the Find what text box type "--" (two dashes), and then press the Tab key to move the insertion point to the Replace with text box. Click the More button to display more options, and then click the Special button at the bottom of the dialog box. Click Em Dash in the list to display Word's special code for em dashes in the Replace with text box. Click the Replace All button. When the operation is complete, click the OK button, and then click the Close button.

23. Add a border to the page using the Page Border command. Click Format on the menu bar, and then click Borders and Shading. In the Borders and Shading toolbox, click the Page Border tab. You can use this tab to customize the border type, line style, color, and width. Select the following options—Setting: Box, Width: 1pt., Apply to: Whole document—and then click OK.

24. Look at the newsletter border in page layout view, using the Whole Page zoom control setting. Center the newsletter contents vertically by adjusting the top margin for the whole document in the Page Layout dialog box.

25. Preview, save, and print the document.

Case Problems

1. City of San Antonio, Texas Blas Rodriguez is the manager of information systems for the city of San Antonio. He and his staff, along with the city manager, have just decided to convert all city computers from the DOS/Windows 3.1 operating system to Windows 95 and to standardize applications software on Microsoft Office 97. Blas writes a monthly newsletter on computer operations and training, so this month he decides to devote the newsletter to the conversion to Windows 95 and to Microsoft Office 97.

1. If necessary, start Word, make sure your Student Disk is in the appropriate drive, and check your screen to make sure your settings match those in the tutorials.

2. Open the file CityComp from the Cases folder for Tutorial 4 on your Student Disk, and then save the file as Computer.

3. Cut the text of the newsletter title, "Focus on Computers." Click the Insert WordArt button on the Drawing toolbar, and then choose the WordArt style in the fourth row, first column. Paste the text (using the Ctrl + V shortcut keys) into the Edit WordArt Text dialog box.

4. In Edit WordArt Text dialog box, set the font to 32 point Arial bold, and apply the Triangle Up shape (top row, third button from the left).

5. Drag the WordArt to the top of the newsletter, and set the wrapping style to Top & bottom in the Format WordArt dialog box.

6. Experiment with changing the shape of the WordArt object by dragging the yellow adjustment handle.

7. Resize the WordArt object so that it spans the width of the page from left margin to right margin and so that its maximum height is about 1 inch. (*Hint:* Use the resize handles while watching the horizontal and vertical rulers in page layout view to adjust the object to the appropriate size.)

8. Center and italicize the subtitle of the newsletter, "Newsletter from the Information Management Office."

9. Insert a continuous section break before the subtitle.

10. To highlight the paragraph with the city name, center the text and then insert a border around all four sides. (*Hint:* Use the Borders button on the Formatting toolbar.)

11. Format the body of the newsletter into two newspaper-style columns, and set the format of the columns so that no vertical rule appears between the columns.

12. Position the insertion point at the beginning of the first paragraph under the heading "Training on MS Office 97," and insert the clip art image from the People at Work category that shows a person talking in front of a group.

13. Resize the picture so that it is 35 percent of its normal size. Instead of dragging the resize handles as you did in the tutorial, use the Size tab in the Format Picture dialog box to scale the image. Adjust the Height and Width settings to 35 percent in the Scale section, and then make sure the Lock aspect ratio check box is selected.

14. Drag the graphic horizontally to the center of the newsletter, and in the Wrapping tab of the Format Picture dialog box, set the wrapping style to Tight, and Wrap to option to Both sides. Make the Left and Right Distance from text .2.

15. Replace any double hyphens with typographic em dashes.

16. Make sure the newsletter fits on one page; if necessary decrease the height of the WordArt title until the newsletter fits on one page.

17. Draw a rectangular border around the entire page of the newsletter. Fill it with a color of your choice, and then use the Draw button on the Drawing toolbar to layer it at the back.

18. If necessary, balance the columns and adjust the newsletter's position on the page.

19. Save and print the newsletter, and then close the file.

2. Federal Van Lines Corporation Martin Lott is the executive secretary to Whitney Kremer, director of personnel for Federal Van Lines (FVL) Corporation, a national moving company with headquarters in Minneapolis, Minnesota. Whitney assigned Martin the task of preparing the monthly newsletter People on the Move, which provides news about FVL employees. Although Martin and others before him have been preparing the newsletter for several years, Martin decides it's time to change the layout and wants to use Word's desktop publishing capabilities to design the newsletter. You will use text assembled by other FVL employees for the body of the newsletter.

1. If necessary, start Word, make sure your Student Disk is in the appropriate drive, and check your screen to make sure your settings match those in the tutorials.

2. Open the file FVL_News from the Cases folder for Tutorial 4 on your Student Disk, and then save it as FVL Newsletter.

3. Change the top and bottom margins to 0.75 inches, and the right and left margin to 1.0 inch. Then insert a blank line at the beginning of the newsletter and apply the normal style to it.

4. Create a WordArt title for the newsletter "People on the Move"; set the font to 24 point Arial bold. Apply the WordArt style in the third row, fourth column from the left, and set the shape of the text to Wave 2 (third row, sixth column from the left).

5. Drag the WordArt title to the top of the newsletter, and set the wrapping style to Top & bottom.

6. Resize the WordArt proportionally so that the title spans the width of the page from left margin to right margin and so that the height of the title is about 1 inch. (*Hint:* Use the resize handles while watching the horizontal and vertical rulers in page layout view to adjust the object to the appropriate size.)

7. Format the body of the newsletter into three newspaper-style columns of equal width and place a vertical rule between the columns. (Remember to use three columns, and not two as you did in the tutorial.) Make sure the rules do not extend through the title object.

8. Position the insertion point at the beginning of the paragraph below the heading "FLV Chess Team Takes Third," and insert the image called "Knight" from the Cases folder for Tutorial 4 on your Student Disk. (*Hint:* Use the same method as you would to insert a clip art image, except instead of selecting Clip Art from the Insert Picture menu, select From File. In the Insert Picture dialog box, go to the location of the file on your Student Disk, select the filename, and then click the Insert button.)

9. Scale the height and the width of the picture to 60 percent of its normal size. (*Hint:* To scale the size, use the Format Picture command, and then set the Scale values on the Size tab, making sure the Lock aspect ratio check box is selected.)

10. Crop 0.3, 0.4, 0.2, and 0.4 inches from the left, right, top, and bottom of the picture, respectively. Use the Picture tab in the Format Picture dialog box, and insert the values in the Crop from text boxes.

11. Drag the clip art to the right side of the center column about 2 inches below the heading. (*Hint:* Select the clip art, and then drag it from the center.)

12. Wrap the text around the clip art.

13. Format drop caps in the first paragraph after each heading. Use the default settings for number of lines, but change the font of the drop cap to Arial.

14. If necessary, decrease the height of the WordArt title until the entire newsletter fits onto one page and so each column starts with a heading.

 15. Add a rectangular border around the entire page of the newsletter using the Page Border command. See the Tutorial Assignments, step 23, for instructions.

16. Save the newsletter, preview, and then print the newsletter. Close the file.

3. Riverside Wellness Clinic The Riverside Wellness Clinic, located in Vicksburg, Mississippi, is a private company that contracts with small and large businesses to promote health and fitness among their employees. MaryAnne Logan, an exercise physiologist, is director of health and fitness at the clinic. As part of her job, she writes and desktop publishes a newsletter for the employees of the companies with which the clinic contracts. She's ready to prepare the newsletter for the October 1998 issue.

1. If necessary, start Word, make sure your Student Disk is in the appropriate drive, and check your screen to make sure your settings match those in the tutorials.

2. Open the file Wellness from the Cases folder for Tutorial 4 on your Student Disk, and then save it as Wellness Newsletter.

3. Change the top and bottom margins to 0.5 inches and the left and right margins to 0.75 inches.

4. At the beginning of the newsletter, create a WordArt title "To Your Health." Choose any WordArt style that you feel would be appropriate to the newsletter content, and set the font to Arial bold, 24 point.

5. Set the shape of the text to any option that looks appropriate to the subject matter.

6. Move the title to the top of the document.

 7. Add a shadow to the WordArt title (or adjust the existing one) by clicking the Shadow button on the Drawing toolbar. Select a Shadow option, and then use the Shadow Settings option on the Shadows menu to select a good color for the shadow. Close the Shadow settings menu. For the purpose of this exercise, choose a shadow style that is behind the text, not in front of it.

 8. Rotate the WordArt 90 degrees. (*Hint:* In the Format WordArt dialog box, click the Size tab and set the Rotation option to 90 degrees.)

 9. Resize the WordArt graphic box so that the WordArt object spans the height of the page from the top margin to the bottom margin, and so that the width of the object is about 1 inch. (*Hint:* Use the resize handles while watching the horizontal and vertical rulers in page layout view to adjust the object to the appropriate size.)

10. Drag the WordArt object to the left edge of the page.

11. Set the Wrapping style to Square, set the Wrap to option to Right, and then change the Right setting under Distance from text to .2".

12. At the top of the page, to the right of the title, italicize the subtitle and the line that contains the issue volume and number of the newsletter.

13. Format the body of the newsletter into two newspaper-style columns with a vertical rule between the columns. (*Hint:* The columns' widths will be uneven because the WordArt title takes up part of the first column space.)

14. To the right of each of the words "NordicTrack" and "HealthRider," insert a registered trademark symbol (®), and then change the font size of the symbol to 8 points. (*Hint:* Highlight the symbol and change the font size.)

15. Balance the columns and if necessary adjust the top margin to center the newsletter vertically on the page.

16. Add a rectangular border around the page using the Page Border command. To do this, follow the instructions in the Tutorial Assignments, step 23.

17. Save the newsletter, preview, and then print it. Close the document.

4. Holiday Greetings Newsletter As a way of keeping in touch with family and friends, a friend suggests that you send out a New Year's greeting newsletter. In the one-page newsletter, you'll include articles about you and your family or friends, recent activities, favorite hobbies, movies, books, and future plans. You'll desktop publish the copy into a professional-looking newsletter.

1. If necessary, start Word, make sure your Student Disk is in the appropriate drive, and check your screen to make sure your settings match those in the tutorials.

2. Write two articles to include in the newsletter; save each article in a separate file.

3. Plan the general layout of your newsletter.

4. Create a title ("New Year's News") for your newsletter with WordArt.

5. Save the document as "New Years News."

6. Insert the current date and your name as editor below the title.

7. Insert the articles you wrote into your newsletter. Open the first article file, select all of the text, copy it, click in the newsletter file at the location where you want it to appear, then paste it. Repeat the procedure for the second article.

8. Format your newsletter with multiple columns.

9. Insert a clip art picture into your newsletter, and wrap text around it.

10. Format at least two drop caps in the newsletter.

11. Create a colored background for the newsletter. Center the contents vertically by adjusting the top margin.

12. Save and print the newsletter.

13. Close the document.

Answers to Quick Check Questions

SESSION 1.1

1. Determine what you want to write about; organize ideas logically; determine how you'll say what you want to say; create your document with Word; edit your document; format your document; print your document.

2. Click Start, point to Programs, click Microsoft Word on the Programs menu or point to Microsoft Office on the Programs menu and click Microsoft Word.

3. a. a ribbon of icons providing menu shortcuts;
   b. bar displaying grid marks every 1/4 inch;
   c. blinking vertical bar indicating where typed characters will appear;
   d. set of characters of a certain shape;
   e. set of standard format settings.

4. Click Format, click Font, select the desired font size, click Default, click Yes.

5. Click View, point to Toolbars, click Standard.

6. Click the Show/Hide ¶ button on the Standard toolbar.

SESSION 1.2

1. You should save a document several times so you don't lose your work in the event of a power failure or other computer problem.

2. Click the Save button on the Standard toolbar. Specify the correct folder and directory in the Save in list box, type the file name in the File name text box, click Save.

3. To display a portion of the document that has scrolled from sight, click the up or down scroll arrows on the vertical scroll bar.

4. Print Preview allows you to see what the printed document will look like. You should use it before printing a document that you have made changes to or when printing a document for the first time.

5. a. shifting or moving the text in the document window to see the entire document one screen at a time;
   b. automatic breaking of a line of text at the right margin;
   c. feature that automatically corrects common misspellings and typing errors;
   d. Help feature that answers questions about current tasks; sometimes appears automatically.

6. Click the Word window Close button.

SESSION 2.1

1   Click the Open button on the Standard toolbar, or click File, click Open, and double-click the file. Click File, click Save As, select the location, type the new filename, click OK.

2   a. Ctrl + End
    b. Ctrl + Home
    c. Ctrl + PageDown

3   Select the text to delete, press Delete.

4   a. The process of first selecting the text to be modified, and then performing operations such as moving, formatting, or deleting on it.
    b. The blank space in the left margin area of the document window, which allows you to easily select entire lines or large blocks of text.
    c. The process of moving text by first selecting the text, then pressing and holding the mouse button while moving the text to its new location in the document, and finally releasing the mouse button.

5   Position the pointer at the beginning of the phrase, press and hold down the mouse button, drag the mouse pointer to the end of the phrase, and then release the mouse button.

    Click in the selection bar next to the line of text you want to select.

6   The Undo command allows you to reverse the last action or set of actions you performed.

    The Redo command allows you to restore a change you reversed using Undo.

7   False.

8   When you use cut and paste, the text is removed from its original location and inserted at a new location in the document.

    When you use copy and paste, the text remains in its original location, and a copy of it is also inserted in a new location in the document.

9   The text will be inserted at the location of the dashed insertion point.

10 Click the Select Browse Object button, click the Find button, click the Replace tab, type the search text in the Find what text box, type the replacement text in the Replace with text box, click Find Next or click Replace All.

SESSION 2.2

1   Align left: each line flush left, ragged right; align right: each line flush right, ragged left; center: each line centered, both ends ragged; justify: each line flush left and flush right; select the text to be aligned or justified, click the appropriate button on the Formatting toolbar.

2   The Format Painter allows you to easily apply the formatting from one block of text to other text.

    Select the text whose format you want to copy, double-click the Format Painter button on the Standard toolbar, click in each paragraph you want to format. When you are done, click the Format Painter button to turn it off.

3   Make sure the insertion point is located in the paragraph you want to indent, and then click the Increase Indent button on the Formatting toolbar once for each half-inch you want to indent.

4   False.

5   Select all the items you wish to bullet, and then click the Bullets button on the Formatting toolbar.

6   Select the text you wish to make bold, and then click the Bold button on the Formatting toolbar.

7   Select the text whose font you wish to change, click the Font list arrow on the Formatting toolbar, and then click the name of the new font on the list.

8   Click the Select Browse Object button, click the Find button, click the Replace tab, type "strategy" in the Find what text box, type "plan" in the Replace with text box, click Replace All.

9   With no text selected, click File, click Page Setup, click the Margins tab, type the new values in the text boxes or click the spin arrows to change the settings. Make sure the Apply to text box displays Whole document, and then click OK.

SESSION 3.1

1   a. a set of formats that can include font, size, and attributes such as bold and italic;
    b. a set of predefined styles designed for a specific type of document;
    c. a list, accessible from the Formatting toolbar, that allows you to apply a style to selected text;
    d. a unit or part of a document that can have its own page orientation, margins, headers, footers, and vertical alignment;
    e. the position of the text between the top and bottom margins;
    f. text that is printed at the top of every page

2   A section break allows you to format different parts of the document in different ways. In the tutorial, the section break you inserted allowed you to create a header that was printed only on pages 2 and 3, and it allowed you to vertically center the text on the first page only.

3   Insert a section break, move the insertion point within the section you want to align, click File, click Page Setup, click the Layout tab, select the center in the Vertical Alignment list box, make sure This section is selected in the Apply to list box, click OK.

4   A header appears at the top of a page, while a footer appears at the bottom of a page.

5   Click the Insert Page Number button on the Header and Footer toolbar.

6   First, attach the template to the document. Then apply the template's styles to the various parts of the document.

7   Click Format, click Style Gallery, click the template you want to preview, verify that you have selected the template you want, click OK.

8   You selected text, clicked the Style list arrow on the Formatting toolbar, clicked the name of the style to apply to the text.

SESSION 3.2

1   Click the place in the document where you want to insert the table. Click the Insert Table button on the Header and Footer toolbar, click and drag to select the numbers of rows and columns you want in your table, release the mouse button.

2   Position the pointer over the border between two columns, click and drag the pointer until the column is the width you want, release the mouse button.

3   d.

4   a. information arranged in horizontal rows and vertical columns; b. the area where a row and column intersect; c. a gray or colored background

5   Click cell A2 or press the Tab key; click cell B6 or press the ↑ key.

6   Click the cell below the column, click the Tables and Borders button on the Standard toolbar, and then click the AutoSum button on the Tables and Borders toolbar.

7   Click in the selection bar to select the row above which you want to insert a row, right-click the selected row, click Insert Rows.

SESSION 4.1

1 (list 3) The printing is high-quality; the document uses multiple fonts; the document incorporates graphics; the document uses typographic characters; the document makes use of columns and other special formatting features.

2 a. a Microsoft Office feature that allows you to design text with special effects;
   b. a square handle you can use to change the size of a graphic;
   c. an arrangement of text using narrow columns that read top to bottom and consecutively from left to right

3 Position the insertion point at the location where you want to create WordArt, click the Drawing button on the Standard toolbar, click the Insert WordArt button on the Drawing toolbar, click the style of text you want to insert, click OK, type the text you want and make formatting selections, click OK.

4 To resize a WordArt object, select the object, drag the resize handles; to resize proportionally, press and hold the Shift key while dragging a handle.

5 The WordArt Shape button allows you to choose the basic shape of a WordArt object.

6 True. Normal view shows each column in its own section; only page layout view, however, shows how the columns appear in the final document.

7 To format text into newspaper-like columns, you use the <u>Columns</u> command on the <u>Format</u> menu.

8 If you want one part of your document to be in two columns, and another part to be in full width, you must insert a <u>section break</u> between the two sections.

9 False. Column formatting will automatically justify the text on each line, but not the lengths of the columns.

SESSION 4.2

1 a. existing artwork that you can insert into your document;
   b. special symbols and punctuation marks that distinguish desktop-published documents;
   c. a large, uppercase letter that highlights the beginning of the text of a newsletter, chapter, or some other document section;
   d. to cut off one or more of the edges of a graphic

2 Position the insertion point at the location where you want to insert the image, click Insert, point to Picture, click Clip Art, click the Clip Art tab, click the category you want to use, click the image you want to insert, click Insert.

3 Resizing leaves the graphic intact but changes its dimensions. Cropping actually removes part of the graphic from view.

4 Click in the paragraph that you want to begin with a drop cap, click Format, click Drop Cap, click the icon for the type of drop cap to insert, select the font, set the appropriate number in the Lines to drop text box, click OK.

5 Click where you want to insert the symbol in the document, click Insert, click Symbol, select the symbol to insert, click Insert.

   ™, ©

6 Make sure that the AutoCorrect feature is set up to replace typing with special symbols; then type text that Word will convert to the symbol you want to insert.

7 Click the Drawing button on the Standard toolbar, click the Rectangle button on the Drawing toolbar, drag to create the rectangle you want to insert, click the Line Style button and select the appropriate style, click the Fill Color list arrow and select the fill color you want to use, click OK.

8 Position the insertion point at the end of the last column you want to balance, click the Zoom Control list arrow on the Standard toolbar, click Whole Page, click Insert, click Break, click the Continuous option button in the Section breaks section, click OK.

Microsoft Word 97 **Task Reference**

TASK	PAGE #	RECOMMENDED METHOD
Border, draw around page	W 4.21	Click Format, click Borders and Shading; on Page Border tab, click Box, apply to Whole Document; see also Rectangle, draw
Bullets, add to paragraphs	W 2.19	Select paragraphs, click ⊞
Clip art, add	W 4.13	Click Insert, click Picture, click Clip Art; click category and image, click Insert
Column break, insert	W 3.4	Click Insert, click Break, select Column Break, click OK
Columns, balance	W 4.20	Click end-of-column marker, click Insert, click Break, click Continuous option button, click OK
Columns, format text in	W 4.10	Select text, click ▦, drag to indicate to number of columns
Date, insert	W 1.13	Click Insert, click Date and Time, click desired format, click OK
Document, create new	W 1.13	Click ▢
Document, open	W 2.3	Click ▣, select drive and folder, click the filename, click OK
Document, preview	W 2.24	Click ▣
Document, print	W 1.22	Click ▣, or click File, click Print to specify pages or copies
Document, save	W 1.16	Click ▣, or click File, click Save As, select drive and folder, enter new filename, click Save
Document window, close	W 1.26	Click ▣ on the document window menu bar
Drop cap, insert	W 4.17	Position insertion point in paragraph, click Format, click Drop Cap, select desired features, click OK
Envelope, print	W 1.25	Click Tools, click Envelopes and Labels, click Envelopes tab, type name and address, click Print
Font size, change	W 2.21	Select text, click Font Size list arrow, click a font size
Font style, change	W 2.23	Select text, click **B**, *I*, or U̲
Font, change	W 2.21	Select text, click Font list arrow, click new font
Footer, insert	W 3.30	Click View, click Header and Footer, click ▣, type footer text, click Close
Format Painter, format paragraph with	W 2.18	Select text with desired format, click ▣, click in target paragraph
Graphic, crop	W 4.15	Click graphic, click ▣, drag resize handle
Graphic, resize	W 4.14	Click graphic, drag resize handle
Header, insert	W 3.7	Click View, click Header and Footer, type header text, click Close
Help, get	W 1.23	Click ▣ and type a question, click Search, click topic

Microsoft Word 97 **Task Reference**

TASK	PAGE #	RECOMMENDED METHOD
Line spacing, change	W 2.29	Click Format, click Paragraph, click Indents and Spacing tab, click Line spacing list arrow, click desired line spacing option, click OK
Margins, change	W 2.14	Click File, click Page Setup, click Margins tab, enter margin values, click OK
Nonprinting characters, display	W 1.10	Click ¶
Normal view, change to	W 1.9	Click [≡]
Numbering, add to paragraphs	W 2.20	Select paragraphs, click [≣]
Office Assistant, open	W 1.24	Click [?]
Page, move to top of next	W 3.9	Click [⬇]
Page, move to top of previous	W 3.9	Click [⬆]
Page, view whole	W 4.11	Click Zoom Control list arrow, click Whole Page
Page layout view, change to	W 3.8	Click [▣]
Page number, insert	W 3.9	Click Insert, click Page Numbers, select location of numbers, click OK
Paragraph, change indent	W 2.17	Select paragraph, drag left or first-line indent marker on ruler; click [≣] or [≣]
Rectangle, draw	W 4.22	Click [⬀], click [▢], drag pointer to draw rectangle
Ruler, display	W 1.9	Click View, click Ruler
Section break, create	W 3.4	Position insertion point at break location, click Insert, click Break, click an option button in Section Breaks section, click OK
Section, vertically align	W 3.5	Move insertion point into section, click File, click Page Setup, click Layout tab, click Apply to list arrow, click This section, click OK
Shading, insert	W 3.27	Click Format, click Borders and Shading, click Shading tab, select Fill and Pattern options, click OK
Spelling, correct	W 1.18	Right-click misspelled word with red, wavy line under it, click correctly spelled word
Style, apply manually	W 3.12	Select text, click Style list arrow, click style name
Style, apply with AutoFormat	W 3.35	Select text, click Format, click AutoFormat, accept or reject proposed changes
Symbol, insert	W 4.18	Click Insert, click Symbol, click desired symbol, click Insert, click Close
Table column width, change	W 3.24	Drag gridline marker on horizontal ruler

Microsoft Word 97 **Task Reference**

TASK	PAGE #	RECOMMENDED METHOD
Table gridlines, display		Select table, click Table, click Show Gridlines
Table, sum cells of	W 3.23	Click sum cell, click Σ on Tables and Borders toolbar
Table row, align text horizontally in	W 3.26	Select a cell or range, click ▤, ▤, ▤, or ▤
Table row, align text vertically in	W 3.27	Select row, click ▦, ▤, or ▤
Table row height, change	W 3.25	Click ▤, drag lower row border
Table row, add or delete borders		Select row, click ▤, ▦, or ▦; to delete click ▦
Table row, delete	W 3.22	Select row, click right-click row, click Delete Rows
Table row, insert at end of table	W 3.22	Position insertion point to lower-right cell at end of table, press Tab
Table row, insert within table	W 3.22	Select row below, right-click row, click Insert Rows
Table, center on page	W 3.32	Select the table, click ▤
Table, insert	W 3.17	Click ▦, drag to indicate number of columns and rows
Table, shade	W 3.27	Select table area, select ▤ on Tables and Borders toolbar
Table, sort		Click Table, click Sort, click Sort by list arrow and select sort column, click sort option button, click OK
Template, attach	W 3.11	Click Format, click Style Gallery, click template name, click OK
Text, align	W 2.16	Click ▤, ▤, or ▤
Text, copy by copy and paste	W 2.11	Select text, click ▤, move to target location, click ▤
Text, copy by drag and drop	W 2.9	Select text, press and hold down Ctrl and drag selected text to target location, release mouse button and Ctrl key
Text, delete	W 1.20	Press Backspace key to delete character to left of insertion point; press the Delete key to delete character to right; press Ctrl + Backspace to delete to beginning of word; press Ctrl + Delete to delete to end of word
Text, find	W 2.12	Click ▤, click ▤, type search text, click Find Next
Text, find and replace	W 2.12	Click ▤, click ▤, click Replace tab, type search text, press Tab, type replacement text, click Find Next
Text, format	W 2.22	See Font Style, change
Text, format automatically	W 3.30	Click Format, click AutoFormat, click OK

Microsoft Word 97 **Task Reference**

TASK	PAGE #	RECOMMENDED METHOD
Text, justify	W 2.16	Click text, click ▦
Text, move by cut and paste	W 2.11	Select text, click ✂, move to target location, click 📋
Text, move by drag and drop	W 2.9	Select text, drag selected text to target location; release mouse button
Text, select a block of	W 2.7	Click at beginning of block, press and hold down Shift and click at end of block
Text, select a paragraph of	W 2.9	Double-click in selection bar next to paragraph
Text, select a sentence of	W 2.6	Press Ctrl and click within sentence
Text, select entire document of	W 2.6	Press Ctrl and click in selection bar
Text, select multiple lines of	W 2.6	Click and drag in selection bar
Text, select multiple paragraphs of	W 2.6	Double-click and drag in selection bar
Toolbar, display	W 1.7	Right-click any visible toolbar, click name of desired toolbar
Word, start	W 1.4	Click Start, point to Programs, click Microsoft Word
Word, exit	W 1.26	Click File, click Exit
WordArt object, insert	W 4.4	Click ◢, click desired WordArt style, type WordArt text, select font, size, and style, click OK